ZAC LEVY

Project Unhoused

A teenager's journey to share the stories of America's homeless

First edition

ISBN: 9798863438702

Editing by Sally Taylor Tawil

This book was professionally typeset on Reedsy.
Find out more at reedsy.com

To my great grandparents, Izzy a"h and Renee Shamah, who have built a stellar family foundation and stitched hesed (good deeds) and emuna (faith) into every cell in my body.

Contents

1

Introduction

You might be thinking to yourself, "Why should I listen to a seventeen-year-old's take on homelessness? He has no experience in the real world. What new insight might he possibly provide to help solve this problem that has existed since the beginning of time?" Now first, that would sting a little, but after asking myself this question, I realized my relative naiveté is more of a blessing than a curse. I view the world through an unadulterated lens. As people age, we get busier and our free time to focus on other pursuits dwindles. While we learn more about the world, we tune it out and focus more and more on ourselves and our place in our community, work, friends, and family. Somehow, we no longer see the homeless man we walk or drive past on our way to work, because we don't have the time to think about what it means or how it makes us feel. That walk or drive is our last break in the morning and the coffee hasn't kicked in yet. Then, on the way home, we are finishing up the day in our head and preparing for the night. For most of us, there is too much going on in our own lives to worry about anything we don't absolutely have to.

Instead, I'd like to introduce you to my world, a world centered around my belief in the absolute interconnectedness and co-responsibility of all people. In this world, homelessness is not something we are okay with; one man's suffering is felt by everyone. In this world, food otherwise thrown in the garbage goes to someone who is starving. In this world, we use our fortunate upbringing as an opportunity to give back and help those who need it. In this world, we shed a tear when seeing the number of people in pain, and we jump at the opportunity to help one person in a tiny way because it will reduce that number. In this world, we can always make a difference if we try. In this world, we try.

Now, the conversation isn't over. Unconvinced by my point, some may protest, "You are wasting your time. Homelessness is caused by a complex mix of mental illness and substance abuse. Leave it to the professionals." I've been told this countless times in many forms, although it is generally veiled by nicer wording, and it always breaks my heart. Almost two-thirds of American adults believe that mental illness and substance abuse are major causes of homelessness, but I've come to view them more as symptoms of a larger problem (1). It is so easy to look at the product of a person experiencing homelessness with serious psychological and substance abuse issues and say it is too late to help. It is much harder to put in the effort to identify the chain of causation that led to the development of said mental health issues and addictions.

The next question is usually, "So you've done all this research, what have you found? What do you think is the primary cause of homelessness?"

"Do you want the long answer or the short answer?" I ask.

Well, if you are here, this is the long answer. Buckle up and let's go back to when it all started.

2

Everything Starts as an Idea

I t was a scorching hot summer day and my father and I were waiting in line at 7/11. As we went to put our two water bottles on the counter, a voice rang through the store. We were pushed to the side by a girl, no more than nineteen, covered from head to toe in cuts and sores with pus oozing out of them. "I'm next in line," she hollered and placed her 99-cent can of Arizona iced tea on the counter. She was grasping onto the counter with one hand while her other hand fished through her pockets searching for some change. She started screaming at the cashier with only short pauses to reinforce her feeble grip on the counter, the only thing preventing her from collapsing onto the floor. I nudged my dad and he ran to the counter and handed his credit card to the cashier and said, "It's on me." Instantly, she bolted out of the store and the only sign of her existence was the bells ringing as my father swiped his credit card. When we left the store, we saw her lying on a bench, surrounded by other homeless people and some meager belongings, chugging her drink. I was filled with compassion and a desire to understand how this teenager, only a few years older than me, ended up in this situation.

From a young age, my parents instilled within me an absolute focus on community service and had gotten me hooked on the drug of helping others. My father, siblings, and I trained to become hospice volunteers, and we were able to spend time with senior citizens in the final stages of their lives. Everyone was so open to talking about their lives, their war stories, the lessons they'd learned, and the things they regretted. We made deep connections with many patients whom we visited weeks in a row and I internalized the idea that you can learn something from anyone who is willing to talk with you.

The core idea behind Project Unhoused stemmed from a fusion of these two formative experiences. I wanted to help the young woman who found herself in such a terrible position at a young age but didn't know how. The gears in my head started spinning. I thought: If I could interview homeless individuals to learn about their life stories and how they had become homeless, I could search for similarities and work to identify some of the root causes of homelessness. That night, over dinner, I told my parents my idea.

By the time we had finished eating, the idea was refined into an action plan. I would work with local restaurants to make punch cards for a few meals that I would sponsor and give to each of the people I interviewed. I would go with my father to known homeless gathering locations and ask people if they were willing to tell us about themselves. From there, I would write all of the stories into a book to share my findings.

While initially this idea seemed perfect, retrospectively, it was impossible. If not for the input of family and friends, you would not be reading this book today. They pointed out tons of details we had overlooked: How would we ensure safety? Would restaurants be willing to participate? Addressing these questions, among many others, was essential towards creating the final rendition of Project Unhoused, a plan that has slowly unwound over the last year. Ultimately, I decided I would partner with local homeless shelters and nonprofits to interview homeless individuals in secure settings. After each interview, I would give the interviewee a Walmart gift card as a thanks for their time. Then, I would collect all of the interviews into a book.

With the idea finalized, I filmed a video recounting the story above and explaining the concept behind Project Unhoused. The next step was going to be harder. I had to open myself up to my community and the internet at large. I created a YouTube Channel, uploaded the video, and started a GoFundMe to fundraise. Over the next month, I texted family, friends, community members, and every single group chat I was in. I made phone calls and Instagram posts, anything to spread the word. Donations poured in from names I knew well and names I had never heard of. In a few weeks, I was able to raise $4,000 which seemed to me like near infinite money. It was time to really get started.

3

The Lay of the Land

After raising money, the next step was to familiarize myself with the landscape and the existing organizations. I searched the internet for all local homeless shelters, soup kitchens, and food banks and read their websites for more information on their operations. Every organization I researched was impressive, but simply reading their website didn't provide me with all the information I had hoped for. I knew I needed to reach out to the leaders of many of these organizations for advice on how to proceed.

The day before I began my junior year of high school, I had my first meeting in Asbury Park with Paul McEvily, the executive director of Interfaith Neighbors. Despite all of my reading, I was completely unprepared. I had never been a part of any sort of meeting before, and if my father hadn't accompanied me, I wouldn't have been able to glean nearly as much useful information as I did. I didn't even remember to take notes. In addition to everything Paul taught me about the nonprofit landscape in Monmouth County, I learned what it was like to participate in a meeting. It would take many more meetings before I fully grasped this material.

Interfaith Neighbors is an amazing organization that does so much for the homeless and near-homeless in Monmouth County. Paul introduced me to all the different branches of the organization and taught me about valuable terminology relating to the homeless and the struggles he's faced throughout his decades working there. His largest focus was the distinction between helping the pre-homeless and the homeless.

Helping the pre-homeless is fundamentally easier and more effective. At this point, you don't need to rebuild someone's life; rather you are providing them the tools to prevent it from falling apart. The near-homeless are in a very precarious position, where one unexpected expense can force them to choose between their rent and their dinner. Paul explained it best through an example: Consider a person whose car engine failed and they don't have the money to repair it. If they don't get this money in time, they can't go to work and then can't afford their rent and food. This cycle can quickly plunge them into homelessness. If an organization can pay this unexpected expense, then they can literally save this family from homelessness.

On the other hand, let us suppose that they were unable to receive the help they needed to fix their car. They tried taking public transportation and asking friends to drive them but ran out of spare cash and favors by the time they would have received their paycheck. Since they couldn't make it to work, they were fired, and it was only a matter of time until they lost their apartment. Months later, an organization tries to help get them back on their feet. The amount of work necessary now is thousands of times more than the cost of fixing that engine. By getting involved earlier in the process, the organization has a much better and more cost-efficient ability to help this family.

For this reason, Paul explained, the majority of Interfaith Neighbors' divisions are focused on aiding the near-homeless. Here are some of the incredible ways they have been able to help the Monmouth County community:

Similar to Habitat for Humanity, Interfaith Neighbors has a large division devoted to building affordable housing. They purchase empty lots or boarded-up houses and build or renovate the houses, then sell them to low-income families at the price of the construction or renovation. To date, they have completed over sixty homes and sold them at way below market values. Within this branch of their organization, they also have a "Rent to Own" program and a Rental and Mortgage Assistance program which are geared towards helping the near-homeless. The former's goal is to enable low-income families to afford a down payment to purchase a home. The latter provides assistance to families that are struggling to pay rent or their mortgage so they don't lose their homes. In order to qualify, one must have dependent children, a full-time job, and live in Monmouth County. Paul spoke of this program with the same pride one speaks of their children: he shared stories about the families they've been able to help and their faces when they first see the miracle of their new home.

Another amazing branch of Interfaith Neighbors is the launch center. Their goal is to meet people at their own level and help them in any way possible. The huge breadth of their programs covers a variety of skill sets and needs, offering workshops in financial literacy and how to balance expenses, interpersonal skills, mental health and wellness techniques, and how to handle yourself in professional environments. They have a program to teach people a trade and provide them employment opportunities in that field as well as a program to provide short-term employment to those who need some extra money. In both of these programs, the goal is to find long-term employment and stable income.

Interfaith Neighbors recently built an innovative hydroponic greenhouse called the Kula Farm. They have a short-term job program where people can earn some extra money and gain practical agricultural experience. Everything they grow is given directly to those in need addressing the huge lack of fresh produce that many food insecure people encounter. They also offer workshops teaching the community about the importance of good nutritional habits.

Through these programs, they cover almost everything that people need. If one qualifies for their assistance, takes advantage of the resources available, and really applies themselves, Interfaith Neighbors is able to catch them before they fall into homelessness. Paul was beyond helpful in laying the foundation for my understanding of the efforts to help the near-homeless. On top of everything else, Paul introduced me to many other local organizations and their missions.

A couple of days later, I met with Linda Curtiss, who runs the Bradley Beach Food Pantry. This time, I came prepared with my notebook and pencil. We pulled into the church's parking lot, and she led us to a small building. Once inside, we walked past her desk, down some stairs, and into a huge basement with aisle after aisle of shelves lined with canned foods. It felt like we walked into a supermarket. They provide food to over three hundred and fifty families five days a week. They keep themselves well-stocked through government aid and donations of money and food. The scale of the operation was mind-blowing. In addition to showing us what a food bank looks like and how it operates, Linda introduced us to many other local charities.

Our next meeting was in Red Bank with Kevin McGee, the Director of Operations at Lunch Break. He showed us around the building and explained their operations. Similar to Interfaith Neighbors, Lunch Break has divisions for almost every single service someone could need. They supply free food, clothes, life skill programs, and health and wellness seminars. At the beginning of the year, they have a Back to School drive, around holiday times they have a Gift Drive, and at the end of the year, they have a Prom Drive. Kevin barely gave us enough time to comprehend the magnitude of their efforts and not nearly enough time to take notes on all of them. We could have spent an entire day together and not even scratched the surface.

After our tour, Kevin asked more about my goals, and as I explained his face lit up. Kevin majored in psychology with a concentration on how childhood trauma affects brain function. He explained that the psychological ramifications of growing up in poverty are lifelong and devastating. Growing up in poverty trains you to only think in the short term. One is so focused on their next meal and where they are going to sleep the next night that they never train the long-term decision-making portion of their brain. Because of this, they often act rashly and without thinking.

My conversation with Kevin prompted me to do more research into this topic; I found that research shows that not only does substance abuse distort the brain's ability to feel pleasure, but it also can lead to abnormalities in the decision-making center, a consequence of which is a lack of foresight. One experiment compared the gambling techniques of people who had drug abuse problems with those who did not and found that about a quarter of the patients who had a history of drug abuse had strategies that were focused on short-term rewards and failed in the long term (2). This is extremely similar to a story Kevin shared with me. At Lunch Break, they have a service where they provide lunch to those who need food. It is not uncommon for people to scream and curse at the staff and storm out after getting their food without realizing that they will need to come back tomorrow.

Kevin explained how there are multiple reasons why the long-term decision-making parts of their brain might be undeveloped. When people grow up in poverty, they can be so focused on the present that they don't have the ability to think ahead. Drug abuse halts natural brain development in adolescents, so many who use drugs from a young age don't have fully developed decision-making processes. Physical and emotional traumas can also affect brain function and development.

By this point, I was feeling more comfortable in meetings. Though

I still struggled to find the right words to express myself and could have worked on my note-taking, I started to find my rhythm. I got along very well with all the people we met because they were such kind-hearted people. Each of them devoted themselves to the nonprofit world because they wanted to help others. Kevin even said at one point that one doesn't make a lot of money in the nonprofit world, but he'd rather help others and make less. At the end of every meeting, I was inspired and invigorated.

Kevin offered to look over the questions that I had prepared to ask at my interviews with people experiencing homelessness. He also offered me the opportunity to conduct interviews at Lunch Break when they have their giveaways every weekday from 11 am and 1 pm. Unfortunately, I had started school and wasn't available at that time, but once the summer started, I took Kevin up on his offer. Kevin also gave me a lot of vital advice about how to conduct an interview and how to be exceedingly sensitive to the feelings of those whom I am interviewing. This advice proved invaluable.

In my next meeting with Phil Richards, Director of the Jersey Shore Rescue Mission, things fully began to materialize. Jersey Shore Rescue Mission is a homeless shelter that does incredible work in Asbury Park. In addition to providing emergency shelter and food, they also offer a Life Change Program to help people overcome substance abuse. From there, these graduates can enter a relapse prevention program, stay at the Sober Living House, or work as an intern to assist the next group. Mr. Richards introduced us to some of these interns, and while we didn't get to speak for long, their outlook on the world was so positive, and their smiles filled the huge room, which would very soon be filled with people who otherwise would have nowhere to sleep and nothing to eat for dinner.

After showing us around, Mr. Richards was ready to set us up for our first interview. People were just starting to arrive where they would be

11

able to shower, have dinner, and spend the night. Unfortunately, I was not yet prepared, so we left it that I would prepare some questions and would email him when I was ready.

My last meeting in this phase of the project was in Asbury Park with Donna Elms, the Program Supervisor at the Winifred-Canright House. The Canright House is a transitional house for men with HIV/AIDS. They provide housing for up to two years and resources to allow the resident to become self-sufficient. By this point, I was comfortable sitting around a big table, taking a tour of the building, and then discussing my project in depth. The meeting went nothing like that. When I walked into the Canright House, introduced myself to Stacy at the front desk, and explained that I was there to meet Donna, Stacy's face glowed as he said, "Donna told us all about your project! We are so excited to be able to help!"

Suddenly, the door opened behind him and Donna rushed out and greeted my father and me with big hugs. We went into her tiny office and she opened up two folding chairs for us. I started to explain my goals the same way I had four times before, but she was way ahead of me. She spoke quickly and excitedly about how thrilled she was that I was doing this at such a young age, showering me with compliments to the point where I didn't know what to say.

It was only minutes into our meeting and she was ready for me to conduct my first interview. She had already chosen a good subject to start with and explained that everyone in the house knew about my project and was willing to be interviewed. Unfortunately, this meeting was only a few days after my meeting with Mr. Richards, and I had not yet finalized the questions. We scheduled a time for a second meeting and our first interview.

For the next half hour, we had a beautiful conversation with Donna about her nonprofit work and my goals with Project Unhoused. As we spoke, I realized just how incredible Donna is. She is currently attending college at night while working a full-time job and taking care of her children. Despite her ridiculously busy schedule, she continues to fill her time with more and more volunteer work and novel ideas to help more people. Donna epitomizes the idea that one can gain more from helping others than what they are giving. She derives so much joy from helping others that she cannot help but share it with everyone around her. She kept repeating that my dedication empowered and recharged her, yet I have never seen Donna functioning at less than 200% of normal energy levels.

In the five meetings I had—Interfaith Neighbors, The Bradley Beach Food Pantry, Lunch Break, Jersey Shore Rescue Mission, and The Winifred-Canright House—I explored many different facets of the problem of homelessness and the different methods organizations use to help. I learned about the importance of preemptive programs, feeding and clothing those experiencing homelessness, relief programs, providing support through basic necessities like food and clothing, and programs designed to help those experiencing homelessness reenter society. I heard stories that made me rethink the path of human development and how formative one's early years are. I met the most kind and generous people who have devoted their entire lives to helping others. I discovered the power of religion and interfaith collaboration to rally people around charitable causes. I owe my utmost gratitude to those who gave up their time to teach me these skills which were critical to Project Unhoused and my development over the last year.

4

Meet Larry

Straight from school, my father and I drove to Asbury Park, parked, and walked into the Winifred-Canright house.

"Good Afternoon Stacy! Is Donna in?"

Before Stacy could answer, the door behind him swung open, "Zac and Izzy!" Donna called, "Come in. Come in." We spoke for a few minutes before Donna went to find Larry. Larry was an average-height middle-aged African-American man with a bit of a beer belly.

"Nice to meet you, Larry," I said. I sensed a certain timidness in his demeanor. He walked somewhat hunched over and avoided direct eye contact. It was difficult to hear what he was saying as he was missing some teeth and spoke quickly without enunciating. Donna directed us to supposedly the quietest room in the house. There were three circular wooden tables spread out with two seats at each. Behind us was the only bathroom on the first floor, and a minor source of disturbance over the next two hours. In the corner was an elderly wheelchair-bound man watching TV whose name we didn't get because he barely spoke a word of English. We didn't want to kick him out, so our conversation was punctuated by the occasional, "GOALLLLL!" followed by a flurry of Spanish I couldn't comprehend.

I pulled over a chair for my father, took out my folder, and told Larry the premise of my project before confirming he was willing to be interviewed. When he was ready, we began with the first of my curated list of questions.

"To start, would you like to tell me a little about your early life?"

Months of reading statistics and articles could not prepare me for this moment. Larry started from the beginning with no sugarcoating, just layers and layers of abuse and trauma. Here it goes.

Larry was born in Camden, New Jersey, in 1972. When he was very young, his family was struck by disaster. Larry's mother was killed while hitchhiking; the driver tried to rape her, and while attempting to flee, she broke her neck and died. He wasn't told this story until he was ten years old.

Larry grew up with his father and stepmother, both of whom were abusive alcoholics. Larry's mind raced between stories of being hit for poor grades, sexually abused by cousins, and rampant drug and alcohol abuse in his community. There was no sense of calm or source of security anywhere in his upbringing, yet he said it all so casually I almost thought I misheard him. He shared a story of his father beating him in front of all his friends at school when he saw his report card. "Ever since that beating," Larry told me, "I had straight A's." I tried to picture Larry in middle school coming into school the next day trying futilely to hide his injuries.

What was even more surprising was that even as he continued to share terrible stories of abuse and neglect, he never said anything besides, "My father was a violent man." He would explain through stories but never was willing to use any negative adjectives besides violent. Even when sharing that his father had murdered someone before he was born, he used no additional adjectives. It was simply a matter of fact.

Later in our interview, he shared that he has bipolar disorder, which he likely inherited from his father. His condition primarily manifests as anger issues, depression, and anxiety. In his mind, Larry absolved his father by blaming the abuse on his father's mental health problems. While bipolar disorder is primarily a genetic condition, it can develop in children as a result of various childhood traumas including neglect, sexual, physical, or emotional abuse, and traumatic events (3). It is possible that Larry's bipolar disorder was caused or strengthened because his father subjected him to these terrible conditions throughout his childhood. Larry explained that his father likely grew up in similar conditions.

At this realization, my heart broke. Not only did Larry grow up in a house where he was constantly afraid that his father would stumble in drunk or high, but he wasn't even able to blame anyone. He associated all his beatings and traumas not with his father, but with his drunk bipolar father who really loved him but couldn't express it. The next morning when his father was calmer and went off to work, there were real bruises and cuts, but he couldn't bring himself to blame anyone. Larry was born into a vicious cycle of mental health issues caused by abuse passed down from his grandfather to his father to him.

From a young age, Larry had a knack for fixing electronic devices, and a love for landscaping, either of which could have provided him a stable career. Instead, when Larry was about to graduate high school, everything took a turn for the worse. Larry had been working at a car wash for a couple of months and was starting to save up some money. Things had only deteriorated at home, so Larry decided to move in with his cousin. A large fight with his stepmother ensued, and although they later reconciled, Larry said some things he really regretted. A couple of nights later, his father called with the news that she was in a coma from alcohol poisoning. She never woke up. Both Larry and his father fell into a deep depression. Larry stopped working at the car wash, and his father lost the house. Now, at seventeen, he was left living with his cousin with no one to fall back on.

By this point in the interview, I was bordering on tears. At my age, Larry had been left practically alone with no parental figures for guidance. How was he expected to figure it out? In his position, I certainly would not be able to. His cousin's girlfriend got him a job at Burger King which he held for the next three months. When he was fired, he survived on government assistance until he graduated high school and moved to Neptune, New Jersey.

The physical and emotional trauma that Larry sustained left him scarred and vulnerable. Drugs offered him an escape from the problems of the real world, and he started smoking weed when he was just sixteen. Like every addiction, it started off small and manageable, but as he gained more independence, the substances grew stronger and his addiction started to take over his life. By the time Larry moved to Neptune, he was smoking crack on a regular basis and funneling every paycheck into fueling his addiction. Soon after, he started working at his local Home Goods. There, he found a community that he fit in with. His supervisor was aware of his anger issues and he got along well with his colleagues. Larry worked there stably for two and a half years before the supervisor he got along with left. His new supervisor kept stressing him out until one day, Larry pushed a cart of merchandise into the revolving doors and stormed out.

After this point, the timeline started to get pretty shaky. At twenty years old, Larry was addicted to drugs and living alone on unemployment. When he made the rash decision to cash in his 401k, his descent into homelessness was quick. He turned to crime to support his addiction and slept in cardboard boxes. Occasionally he would stay by other people for brief periods, but overall he spent the majority of a decade on the streets and in jail.

At one point, Larry recovered long enough to find a stable job again for ten months at Bed Bath & Beyond until he was fired when management learned about his criminal record, even though he was transparent about it to his supervisor. That was the last time he worked a job. The rest of Larry's life would follow a similar cycle: Larry would panhandle or steal money to buy drugs, eventually be arrested, serve his time, and return to the streets. Any money he obtained legally was through government programs or donations.

He shared some stories from the latter portion of his life, but by the end, his voice was a near whisper and his eyes were tearing up. He ended by explaining that all the people he mentioned had since passed or he hadn't seen in decades. In the last few years, he'd lost four really close friends to fentanyl poisoning. As I understand it, in order to reduce the cost and increase the potency and addictive capabilities of their products drug dealers have recently been adding fentanyl (a drug 50 times stronger than heroin) deceptively to other drugs. Just two milligrams of fentanyl is deadly, and drug dealers often add more than that amount accidentally or purposefully (4).

Decades on the streets had taken a huge toll on Larry's body. The catalyst for his stay at the Canright House was his worsening heart issues, arthritis, dental problems, asthma, and broken foot. Additionally, Larry is HIV-positive and hadn't been taking his medication for six months. As his health worsened, he realized that if he didn't change, he was likely going to die. At the time of our interview, Larry had been at the Canright House for eleven months. His foot has recovered and he had some teeth removed. He is on medication for his bipolar disorder, depression, anxiety, heart problems, and HIV. When we last spoke, he was applying for housing, hopeful to get a place of his own.

Looking back, Larry said, "I wasted my life… with all the money I've been panhandling and stuff, you know how much money I've made, probably millions." He understands that at his age, this is his last chance to fix things. He has a sponsor and frequently attends AA and NA meetings. I did notice that some of Larry's answers were very vague. When I asked what he is doing differently this time compared to the last time he was at the Canright House in 2006 and stayed sober for three and a half years, he avoided the question. Later he did mention that the reason he relapsed was because he doesn't like to be alone. His solution was to keep himself busy. Once he gets his own place, he wants to dedicate the rest of his life to community work. After all the beautiful things that people did for him during his hard times, he wants to try to make a similar impact on others.

For the last portion of the interview, we reflected back on some of the stories he shared about his life and tried to brainstorm what things, if changed, could have helped Larry. One idea that stood out was the problem of medication. If throughout his life Larry had access to bipolar medication, he would have avoided so many of the pitfalls he fell into. Larry's temper ruined friendships, his relationships with peers, and employers, and landed him in prison on multiple occasions. If his father had been medicated, his entire childhood would have been turned on its head. He might have grown up in a house he felt safe in and with parents who could give him support. The problem was not solely mental health, but rather a failure to diagnose these problems and the lack of access to proper treatment.

After the bulk of the interview was complete, I asked Larry various questions which I thought would be interesting to include.

When asked what he would do to reduce homelessness if he had the power to change things, Larry's major suggestion was more affordable housing, and shelters.

Larry has a slogan that he uses to put the past behind him: "Let go and let God." This is exactly what he did with his feelings about his father. He let go of the hate and resentment from his childhood because it was only weighing him down. Larry left the matter up to God and moved on.

When asked what the biggest compliment he ever received was, Larry spoke about how it came from the staff at the house. When he first arrived at the Canright House, he had frequent outbursts and didn't get along well with the other guys. Since then, he has built camaraderie with his housemates and the staff has noticed and pointed it out to him.

When the pandemic started, Larry recounted that no one ever had formally explained to him what was happening. Suddenly, the streets grew empty and anyone who was outside was wearing a mask. Larry contracted Covid-19 very early on and went to the emergency room. There were no verified treatments at the time, so the doctors just told him to stay hydrated and let the virus run its course. Thankfully, he survived, and for the rest of the pandemic, he wore a mask and gloves and continued his life like normal.

When asked what he would want to tell the whole world if he could say something, he said he would tell everyone to be strong and not to give up. He said, "It's gonna get better... You may go through some bad times or good times, but it's gonna, you just gotta be patient, that's all." This is the same advice he said he would give to a younger version of himself.

The last question I asked was, "What is the most important lesson you've learned?" He responded, "Loving myself." Larry has led an unimaginably hard life, but despite such adversity, he maintains a remarkably positive attitude. Throughout the whole interview, Larry maintained a huge smile and blew me away with his hopes for the future. The way he was able to truly forgive the abusers of his past and sincerely "let go and let God" is astonishing.

5

Winter Clothing Drive

Over the course of the next few weeks, I continued to brainstorm different ways that I could expand my efforts. One idea I was really intrigued with was collecting winter clothing. In our interviews, I noticed that stories of adversity while experiencing homelessness kept beginning with, "It was really cold out one night..." An estimated 700 people experiencing homelessness die each year from hypothermia (5). In my research, I learned that there is a policy adopted in many states called Code Blue. When temperatures are below freezing, a Code Blue alert is publicized, and warming centers across the county or state open up. These warming centers may be in shelters, libraries, hospitals, municipal buildings, or religious centers. At these times, shelters take in as many people as possible and disregard their normal admission process. Everyone bands together to save the lives of those experiencing homelessness. One problem is that hypothermia can be fatal at temperatures 10-15 degrees higher than the cut-off temperature (6). Additionally, the warming centers are scattered about and it can often be difficult to find one.

This problem is difficult to solve from a legislative perspective because it requires the upheaval of all admission rules in shelters, so it is only instituted in emergency situations when extremely low temperatures are reached. Each shelter must institute rules for the safety of those in the shelter; if the entire winter was considered an emergency, there would effectively be no rules. As a result, many experiencing homelessness have to try their best to bundle up and keep warm on slightly above-freezing nights.

We were approaching winter quickly and I figured I could collect winter clothing and blankets to distribute to those in need. Unsure as to how exactly to go about the distribution portion, I started planning the collection. First, I prepared a digital flyer with a brief explanation, my phone number, and a drop-off address. I sent the flyer to all the group chats I was on, posted it on Instagram, and spread the word however I could. Then, I made a physical version which I printed out and started hanging up in local community institutions. My father drove me to the butcher, supermarket, and community center, and I went to the front desk at each and asked if I could hang up the poster. A dozen stores later, the phone calls and texts began. Over the next few weeks, people dropped off bags and my father and I drove to houses to pick them up and I had the pleasure to meet many incredibly kind-hearted and generous people.

Over those months, I accumulated many heartwarming stories. Very early into this process, I got a voicemail from an unknown number during school, "Hello, my name is Mark… I have some coats to drop off… Call me back…" When I got home, I called him and introduced myself. He told me he had some women's coats to drop off and that he would come by this weekend. That Saturday, after my family and I had finished our Shabbat lunch, we heard a knock on the door. Mark introduced himself and handed us two bags filled with beautiful fur coats. My mother and I spoke to Mark for about fifteen minutes and he shared with us how his girlfriend had lost her battle with cancer and only now was he emotionally ready to part with her belongings. I thought it was so beautiful that rather than selling these beautiful fur coats of hers, he wanted to donate them to help others, and it seemed to give Mark a lot of closure that they were going to a good cause.

In no time, the storage space in my garage was cut in half. We started planning our first distribution but still had a number of concerns. Miraculously, all our problems melted away in a chance encounter.

6

Meet James Alai

The school day before the second interview had left me somewhat drained. We had a chemistry lab that day in which we learned how to use Bunsen burners. My group had trouble lighting the burner and continued to increase air and gas flow, thinking that would solve the problem. When it finally lit, the fire was very large; although I jerked my hand back immediately, the hair on two of my fingers burned off. I was unharmed but came out of school extremely spooked. I really did not feel prepared for an interview.

When we walked into the Canright House, Stacy told us that Donna was out. While we waited for him to call her, one of the members of the house walked in and we introduced ourselves. He was an extremely pleasant middle-aged man named Manny. Donna had already told him about Project Unhoused and he was excited for his turn to speak with us.

In the meantime, Stacy had reached Donna and told us our next interview was going to be with James. Stacy showed us to the room where we had met with Larry just a few weeks earlier, then escorted James to where we were waiting. We introduced ourselves, shook hands, and I quickly explained the project before we began the interview.

In our first interview, as soon as I asked one question, Larry had jumped into his life story which he had clearly shared many times before. He had some key points he wanted to focus on at the start, and then for the rest of the interview, I asked questions to fill in blanks and uncover details. On the other hand, with James, it was apparent that he was not nearly as institutionalized as Larry was. He had never grown comfortable telling people his life story. As a result, I had to steer the interview a lot in the beginning.

James was born in New Brunswick, NJ, on Christmas Day in 1987, and is the oldest among his siblings: Joe, Zach, and Haley. His father was a hard-working man, but was as James put it, "a mean guy." He was never physically abusive, but was verbally abusive and would often lose control of himself in fits of rage. He would drink after work and James vividly remembers hiding when his father came home until he figured out his mood. When his father was angry, he would flip over the dinner table or pull the phone out of the wall. For these reasons, James' family was very different when his father was home than when he was at work, and they never had a cohesive family unit. Only on nights when his father worked late did he truly feel comfortable at home.

That's not to say his father was all bad; James does have many memories of fun times with his dad. They bonded through music and would sometimes go to concerts together. James' fondest memories with him are during the summers when they went on camping trips with their cousins. James would also help his father with work and running errands. Overall though, these memories were overshadowed by negativity and James blocked them out as attempt after attempt to love his father was met with apathy or criticism.

James' mother was on the other end of the spectrum. She showered her kids with love and always had a smile on her face. She thought that they could do no wrong and would give up her life for them. His mother was the beacon of light in his life. Throughout our interview his admiration for her was evident and he called her an angel, saint, sweetheart, and the most caring person he knows. Of course, that didn't mean she didn't have her challenges. James' mom suffered from depression and agoraphobia, meaning she rarely went too far from home. They would often go to the mall on weekends, but his mom would never take them further than that. Because of these limitations, she developed a dependence on her husband. She would never rebuke him for drinking too much or smoking. As James put it, "She kind of hung on to my father like he was a lifeline, which is common in abusive relationships."

James went to middle school in South River, but as his father's business did better, they moved to a nicer area in Monroe Township and he switched from Catholic school to Monroe High School. From a very young age, James had a passion for filmmaking. He used to watch award shows and pretend he was up there speaking. When he moved, he joined his school's film club and would do news broadcasts and make short movies with friends. He even started a YouTube channel that gathered over 100,000 views per video. His dream was to pursue a career in filmmaking. This was the path he was on until his parents got divorced in his senior year. His father gave his mother no money and James' dream had to be thrown out the window. Instead of film school, James attended community college for one year before dropping out to work and help his mother pay the bills.

James worked at various fast-food chains until he found a close-knit community at Applebee's. He started working as a host, then later as a server. There he had his first long-term girlfriend and made some of his closest friends. After the divorce, his mother started working as a barber. James' brother, Joe, had started doing drugs in high school and was in the throes of addiction during this time period. James' youngest brother, Zach, was in high school and had some trouble with drugs before becoming a born-again Christian. James grew very close with him and was involved in his recovery. At this point, James' life was by no means without struggle, but things were okay. He had a great relationship with his siblings and mom, a stable income, a shared apartment with his family, and a great social life. In the span of a couple of months, this all capsized around him in a series of unfortunate events.

When James turned twenty-one, he started to drink, but only socially. He would go to parties and bars with friends but didn't let it take over his life. One night, he was at the bar with his friends when someone approached him and asked for a cigarette. When he started searching through his pockets, the man sucker-punched him, took his wallet, and ran. He woke up on the ground, made his way home, and immediately his brother rushed him to the hospital. His entire jaw was shattered. The hospital wired his jaw shut and gave him liquid morphine for the pain. While he was recovering, he took some time off from his job.

Only a few weeks later, James had an argument with his brother, Zach, over who should drive to Pennsylvania. In the end, Zach relented and drove instead of James. In a tragic car accident, Zach and four others were killed. James lost all faith in God and fell into a deep depression. Even after his jaw recovered, James continued to use liquid morphine as a crutch. When he ran out, his brother Joe informed him that heroin was way cheaper and accomplished the same thing.

Two months later, Superstorm Sandy hit and their apartment was flooded. "I just stopped caring," he said, "I didn't want to feel, you know." Three tragic disasters in quick succession destroyed his life. Soon after he lost his job and his addiction set in roots.

In a matter of months, James lost everything he had. With his jaw injury, he lost his independence. He was forced to rely on his mother for help whom he knew was already overloaded. Furthermore, he was isolated from all his friends at work. With the loss of his brother, James lost his enjoyment of life. The morphine numbed his mind and became his new best friend. Superstorm Sandy added insult to injury. Now he was not only a physical and emotional wreck, but his family's financial situation became unstable. James' mother relied on him to help support their family, and he just couldn't do it. He fell apart.

James spent the next ten years doing drugs, mostly heroin and cocaine, drinking, and finding shelter wherever he could. He would hop between rehabs, psychiatric wards, and his mother's new apartment. Occasionally, James would run out of money and find a job, but quickly the pains of withdrawal would bring him back to drugs and he would call out of work. "I was unemployable," James explained, "I couldn't stick with one thing cause all I wanted money for was for drugs." There is a Narcotics Anonymous saying, "We lived to use and used to live" (7). This is exactly what the drugs reduced James to.

Throughout this entire period, James managed to avoid being arrested for drug use; his criminal record is clean. This is an important detail because it is so difficult for people with criminal records in America to find employment or housing. There are over 40,000 legal collateral consequences of conviction, of which 72% affect employment opportunities (8). What is even more upsetting is that many with criminal records are banned from low-income housing and many landlords upcharge them exorbitantly or won't rent to them at all. Formerly incarcerated people are ten times more likely to become homeless than those without criminal records, and ex-convicts who are able to find stable housing are significantly less likely to commit other crimes (9).

These problems led to a cycle that I became very familiar with throughout this project: the revolving door of incarceration. People fall into poverty, steal or sell drugs to survive, are arrested and serve their time, and then are dumped right back onto the streets where they started. James was thankfully able to avoid the incarceration portion of this cycle.

There is a movement known as Ban the Box that has been making amazing advancements in many states, including New Jersey, to eliminate questions about criminal history during interviews and minimize the weight of minor offenses in the job application process. Similar legislation is being established with regard to housing. Additionally, depending on severity, crimes committed many years ago are being discounted. These measures are aimed to rectify this disparity and end the cycle of recidivism.

It took hitting rock bottom for James to finally seek serious help. When his grandmother moved in with his father, James' father allowed him to live in the grandmother's house until they sold it, on the condition that he would clean it out. James agreed and ended up alone, far from home, without any money. He couldn't afford any drugs and was so sick from withdrawal that he was suicidal. James overdosed multiple times in that house, but thankfully managed to survive.

After this episode, his mother met Carla, a former drug addict who had turned her life around and was trying to help others. Miraculously, Carla was able to get through to James. She drove James to rehab, brought him to the doctors, found him a place at the Canright House, and is taking care of his cats. James has been clean for the last six months thanks to Carla, his mother, his family's support, and his own incredible efforts.

James explained that when one is on drugs they cannot think straight. They cannot even acknowledge that they have a problem. Only now that James has been clean for six months can he start to sift through the last ten years and work through his problems. In our meeting, I found that James was extremely in touch with his feelings and aware of his mistakes. While it was clear he had not told his life story in a format like this before, it was equally clear that he had spent hours and hours reliving the past and digging deeper into his traumas.

Looking back now, James acknowledges that his biggest regret is what he put his mother through. She depended on him for rent and he just left her. She had never encountered something like his situation; when her husband was addicted to alcohol, he still supported his family and kept a stable job. She handled James in the only way she knew how. She never gave him money, knowing he would spend it on drugs. She would occasionally house him, but if he was ever high she would call the police on him. At the time James hated how she treated him, but now he realizes that this was the best approach. She loved him so much she couldn't stand to see him die in front of her.

Now, James goes to meetings at least four times a week, is currently looking for a sponsor, and is starting to see a therapist. Since James doesn't have a criminal record, he has an opportunity to rebuild his life. He recently won a housing lottery and hopes to move out and attend college and study film. James' drive to rebuild his life after such hardship is inspiring. He has such high aspirations and I truly believe that he will achieve great things.

Toward the end of the interview, I asked James some assorted questions which I thought would be interesting to include.

James contracted HIV by using a dirty needle while he was in California visiting his brother and it was a huge wake-up call for him. For the rest of his life, he would have to live with the virus. Some of the symptoms of HIV include depression and anxiety which only advanced James' mental health issues (10). Fortunately, James is on medication for it now and is healthy and undetectable. With modern medicine, people with HIV can live a long and healthy life.

I asked James what he would say if he could talk to a younger version of himself and he gave a beautiful response. He answered, "The hole is never too deep for you to climb out of, and you don't need to dig that hole to begin with." I think this advice can be vital for all of us.

James was actually only homeless for a few weeks. He explained that when he was in Trenton he went to The Salvation Army there. They had a program in which people would work nine hours a day in return for housing and meals. After working for a certain amount of time, they would graduate from the program and be paid minimum wage. James thought the program was outrageous and figured he would be better on his own. He tried staying in a shelter for one night but was absolutely disgusted by the conditions. He showered with a hose, wasn't given a towel, and then slept with his head down on a wooden table surrounded by people using drugs. He decided it would be better to sleep on the streets. For the next week, James slept on the streets and walked around panhandling during the day. He made upwards of one hundred dollars a day until he found a place to stay.

James discovered during the decade that he was jumping between shelters and rehabs that people could be incredibly self-serving. They would do things for others only in return for a favor and there was very little loyalty. Theft was common and you would never know when someone you trusted might disappear along with some of your possessions. James explained that the addicts he met were often extremely smart; in order to survive on their own, they had to be.

Being an avid reader and writer, James used poetry to express himself and his depression. He shared his poetry blog with me and I was able to read some of his poems from his decade of drug use. This was his only outlet for his frustration and anger, and reading through his poems allowed me to briefly see the world through his eyes. Here is one of the poems:

Have you ever felt alone?
Like you are the only one in a crowded room?
You have hopes and dreams tucked away,
in a safe deep inside. And you just stand there and vegetate.
You hide in the corner and sip your drink
while everyone converses about stupid things.
There is a girl who looks at you.
Maybe she is the one you dream about,

the one who can open that safe and let it all spill out.

Your eyes meet. She is everything you need.

But you look down and bite your lazy tongue.

Because you are lonely. Because you are no fun

The walls close in on you.

What did you do?

Nothing.

Nothing at all. (11)

Over the last six months, James has slowly been rebuilding his relationship with his family. His mother is still very reserved and is guarding herself in case he relapses, but they are in touch often now. James' brother Joe has been able to overcome his drug addiction and now lives in California. He is a life coach and runs a successful self-help YouTube channel. His sister, Haley, is studying to be a nurse. She learned from the addiction problems of her siblings and has never touched a drink. James calls his siblings often and is finding his way back into their lives.

The last question I asked James was, "What is something you want to say to the world?" He answered that when people see drug addicts or people on the streets begging for money, they should understand that these are people too, and that they need help. They wouldn't be in this position if they had a choice. His second piece of advice was that parents shouldn't be afraid to have difficult conversations with their children about homelessness and substance abuse.

In the middle of our interview, we heard some commotion in the other room. Someone screamed, "Who threw away the carrots? Those were my carrots!" My dad and I exchanged a nervous chuckle and the interview continued. Over the next ten minutes, we heard the speaker question everyone who walked by about his carrots. He seemed very upset, so when we finished our interview with James, we ran to the nearest grocery store, bought a bag of carrots, and came back. We told

Stacy what happened and he went to get Manny, the man we had met on our way in. His face was red with embarrassment, but he thanked us profusely for the gesture. This is only the beginning of the carrot story, stay tuned.

After the interview, I emailed Donna asking if we could interview Manny next. Unfortunately, she responded that he was "on probation." I didn't ask for more details. She also mentioned that the Canright House had started a program of alumni events. The idea is that people who graduated from the house and were able to successfully rebuild their lives return to check in with everyone and talk about their struggles and how they were able to beat the odds. Unfortunately, we missed the inaugural event, but we committed to attending the next one.

7

A Chance Encounter

O n our way to the Canright House to attend the alumni event, my father and I stopped by a local Dunkin' Donuts so we wouldn't walk in empty-handed. It was nearing closing time, and the shelves were almost empty. All that was left were two donuts and about fifty Munchkins. We started talking to the woman behind the desk and she was incredibly nice. She offered us a free donut as they were about to close and she didn't want them to go to waste. We ordered twenty-five Munchkins, and she generously gave us the full fifty for half price.

While she was filling the bag, she asked what the occasion was and I began to explain my project. When she turned around to hand us the Munchkins she was beaming. "I have been serving this community for the last seven years." She explained, "This Friday, I will be starting a soup kitchen…" We talked for a few minutes about how she dreams of starting a women's homeless shelter because that need is really not being met. It was so nice to meet such a like-minded person! Unfortunately, I couldn't volunteer at her soup kitchen because it would conflict with school hours.

Before we left, I told her that I had been collecting winter clothing to distribute to the homeless, and she offered to help us with the distribution. We exchanged phone numbers and then I brought the Munchkins to the Canright House. Who would have thought that a random interaction at Dunkin' Donuts could be so fruitful? Cherry has been such a help throughout my journey, and in my mind, this meeting was undoubtedly divinely guided. When you put good out in the world, good comes back to you.

8

First Canright House Alumni Event

My father and I walked in a few minutes late from our encounter with Cherry but with big smiles and two boxes of munchkins. Every chair in the living room was taken, so someone ran to a different room and found two chairs. Donna started the night off by introducing us to the group and explaining our efforts. Then, everyone went around in a circle and introduced themselves. There were about a dozen men, including the two whom we had interviewed. Donna then handed it over to the two alumni, Omar and Dennis, to speak.

Omar began with a powerful recounting of his experiences with the Canright House. After being stuck in a cycle of homelessness, drug use, and incarceration for decades, he made a decision that he couldn't live that life anymore. Omar came to the Canright House and was greeted with open arms. After thriving for almost a month, his dedication was tested. He got a phone call that his mother was on her deathbed. Someone drove him to the hospital and he was able to be by his mother's bedside as she passed in her sleep. Before she died they had a conversation that Omar shared with us. It left me on the verge of tears. His mother asked him, "Is it true that you aren't doing drugs anymore?" He answered yes, and she passed away content knowing that after years of worry, her boy was finally safe.

After the funeral though, he was absolutely distraught. Devastated by the loss and withdrawal pains, he was itching to go back to the streets. Omar explained that he had one foot out the door when his friends at the Canright House consoled him and gradually he regained his strength. If not for them, he said, he would never have made it to this point. Afterward, Omar kept his word to his mother. He fully dedicated himself to getting help. He practically glued himself to the phone in the hallways on the second floor as he called every organization in the state. He never watched TV or played games. Instead, he devoted every minute he had to getting the help he needed.

Omar's message was that to overcome these struggles with alcohol and drugs, which everyone in the Canright House is fighting day in and day out, there is a mix of teamwork and selfishness. Within the house, there must be a sense of camaraderie. Everyone has to be there to pick someone up if they stumble. That is essential, but the hardest work has to be done by the person himself. You have to put every effort into exploring the opportunities available to you and making sure you get them. You need to fill out hundreds of forms and make hundreds of calls. Without the individual's hard work, there won't be any success.

After Omar's poignant speech, Dennis took the floor. Dennis was a drug dealer for decades. Originally, he was so notorious that the Canright House wouldn't even admit him. After spending a few months in an in-between-house building his credibility, Dennis was finally admitted and turned his life around. Since fighting his own demons, Dennis attended college and is now an addiction counselor. What an incredible success story!

Dennis drilled deeper into the psychological war against addiction. He talked about how important it was for everyone to attend meetings and really self-reflect on their goals when they leave the house. Building on what he spoke about, Dennis circled back to an assignment he had given the group at their last meeting. He had asked them to focus on a personal issue and how they were working on it.

James was the first to speak and really opened up to the crowd. He explained that the skill he was working on was learning to take constructive criticism better. James understands that everyone in the house is trying to help each other, but sometimes when others give him advice he gets very angry and lashes out. While the intent behind the comment may be pure, he feels judged and offended. He shared a short story from earlier in the week where he normally would have reacted aggressively, but he thought before he acted and handled himself appropriately. He wants to constantly keep in mind that everyone in the house is on the same team.

Larry was next in line. It was clear he hadn't planned what to say. He hesitated for almost a minute without saying much, then sat up and talked about how his goal is to give back and that he has been looking for opportunities. Then he stopped talking and hoped Dennis would move on, however, Dennis was not fooled; he pushed a little harder for specific actionable steps he took to "work on himself." Larry had no real answer. He just talked about how he goes to meetings and eventually, Dennis stopped pushing as he had made his point.

After Larry, a man whose name I didn't catch spoke beautifully and personally about his fears regarding starting a family. Being HIV positive has weighed heavily on him, and after his wife passed years before, he doesn't think he will ever be able to find another companion. Since the Canright House is specifically for HIV-positive men, this was a struggle that everyone in the room was dealing with. While they are on medication that prevents HIV from majorly affecting their health, it is a huge obstacle in their social lives and relationships. He opened up my eyes to the long-term impacts of the unsanitary conditions on the streets. It hit me that even if everyone in the room made a full recovery mentally, physically, and economically, and their criminal record was erased, the lasting effects of HIV would still make their return to society painful. The stigma associated with HIV is so strong that before our first interview, my father asked me to look up whether or not it would be dangerous to shake the house members' hands. While he was talking I saw everyone nodding their heads and at the end, Dennis walked over and put his hand on the man's shoulder.

A couple of other men spoke afterward, but I had not met them before and didn't memorialize their responses. Additionally, many people hadn't been at the last meeting and didn't know about the assignment. After everyone finished, Omar and Dennis said some parting words, thanked everyone for opening up, and reminded everyone that each day is a struggle and it only takes one mistake to demolish months, or even years, of hard work. We stayed for another few minutes and talked to the people we knew until they served dinner and people started to sit down to eat.

In school, we utilize a style of discussion called a Socratic Seminar in which everyone sits in a circle and discusses a topic in a civil way such that everyone has an opportunity to present their opinions. This experience showed me the real power of such a configuration. Everyone had their time in the limelight to talk about themselves while everyone else listened and gave "uh huh"s and "that's right"s of support. Usually, it can be intimidating to stand up and give a speech to a dozen people, but this arrangement was so laid back that everyone was comfortable sharing. I had the privilege to be a fly on the wall during this meeting and go from learning about these men's past to seeing how they are growing in the present. In the meeting, they touched on their everyday struggles to stay sober and be happy. That night gave me such insight into their lives beyond what I learned in the interviews.

9

First Distribution

We scheduled our first distribution with Cherry for the Sunday after we had first met. When it came time, we loaded up the car with bags and bags of winter clothing and drove to Cherry's housing project. Before we even arrived, there was a line of a dozen people. They helped us unload the car, which was much appreciated as I had sprained my ankle earlier in the week and was wearing a boot.

We had planned to have the distribution outdoors, but it was raining. Instead, we used the community room of Cherry's housing project and set up three tables in the center. On either side, there was a big table with some office chairs as well as a bookshelf and an old computer. There were already a few people congregated inside waiting for us to set up. Cherry, my father, and I started opening the bags and sorting them into stacks of coats, blankets, pillows, sheets, hats, gloves, etc... Before we had even finished opening and organizing everything, a quarter of our stock was gone.

Over the course of the next two hours, people continued to stream in. We would approach them, ask what they were looking for, and help them find what they needed. I started to notice that whenever anyone came in, they would instantly gravitate to Cherry, and avoid eye contact with my father and me. I felt like an outsider. There were a couple of very nice people I had the opportunity to speak with, but without Cherry, I don't think we would have been nearly as successful. She seemed to know almost everyone in the building and they all went on and on about how Cherry helped them. We could not have been gifted with a better partner!

When we left, my father and I spoke about the atmosphere in the building. It felt so amazing to be able to help so many people in need and everyone we spoke to was so appreciative, but I felt a tinge of distrust looming in the air. Looking back, this was one of the only times I felt this way throughout my journey.

10

Meet Carlos

When we got to the Canright House, Donna introduced us to Carlos and we went back to our interviewing room and sat down. Carlos started by showering us with compliments. He said he thought we were siblings, not father and son, and applauded my efforts. At the time he seemed very genuine to me.

Carlos was born in 1959 in Puerto Rico but has lived in New Jersey for as long as he can remember. He lived with his father, nine half-siblings, and various women depending on who his father was currently with. His mother had been out of the picture since he was young. His father told him she was dead and that she had tried to abort him. His siblings perpetuated the lie because "what father said goes." He would tell all his children that he was both their father and mother and would beat them if they couldn't accept that. He was always drinking and looking for a reason to beat his kids. Carlos remembers he would put on multiple layers of clothing when he got home to protect himself from his dad's frequent beatings. He never felt a sense of camaraderie with his half-siblings, as they would always snitch on him to their father and gang up on him. Carlos later explained that he yearned for any form of attention. He found it was easier to get bad attention than good attention.

Carlos always struggled in school. He would act up when his teachers would try to discipline him and didn't complete his classwork or homework. He was failing most of his classes, and when report card season came around, he would run away from home out of fear of his father's inevitable reaction. Carlos went to court many times accusing his father of child abuse, but eventually, he would return home and the beatings would resume.

At age thirteen, Carlos dropped out of school and started drinking and doing drugs. This cycle of running away and returning home continued and Carlos used drugs to numb himself to the pain. He was forced into a position where the only way forward was through stripping himself of his emotions and simply existing. Pain and torment washed over him as he spent every waking moment searching for drug money and developing his reputation as someone you would not want to mess with.

That same year, he went to his first foster home. All he remembers is that their daughter taught him how to drive and after three weeks, he stole their car and drove home. He exhibited no regret that he took advantage of the family's kindness. He saw them as weak and took advantage of them for his gain. The next time he ran away, which wasn't long after, he was sent to the Jamesburg Training School for Boys for five months. He continued to be housed in various reformatories and juvenile detention centers while drinking and using drugs.

When Carlos was fifteen, his brother, Cruz, pulled him aside and shook his world. "Look, I've got something to tell you, but you cannot tell Pop," Cruz said, "your mother's alive." Carlos was baffled. Cruz brought Carlos to her house and introduced him to his mother and an additional thirteen half-siblings. Carlos didn't cry. He pretended to be so excited to see his mother. He told us, "I had no feelings. I had no emotions. But I was playing the street game. I was already a master manipulator." He played along as she hugged him and kissed him while he schemed for ways to get drug money out of their relationship. The drugs had taken over his mind to the point that they were his sole source of motivation. He truly did not care about anything else. He continued to visit her until his father found out and put an end to it.

By this point, I was starting to question how trustworthy Carlos really was. When telling stories, he kept reaching over and touching my arm. I realized that the compliments at the beginning were very likely him trying to butter us up before the interview. He said at one point about his childhood, "I like to talk about this. They do stuff like this with a psychiatrist when you're in prison." He has been so institutionalized over the last five decades that this exercise didn't affect him one bit. He was talking about how he didn't have any feelings back then, but it was clear that fifty years later he engages with the world in exactly the same way. He was saying he did things wrong only because psychiatrists had told him it was wrong. I got the impression that if he was able to go back and relive these moments, he wouldn't change a thing.

Right around when Carlos turned sixteen, he was at the Monmouth County Youth Detention Center and his grandma came to visit him to break the news that his mother had died from cancer. He went to the funeral only because it meant a day out of juvie. He still remembers that day, not because his mother died, but because he was checking out his female cousins and savoring each hug. That's what he remembers from his mother's funeral. He had no feelings of loss. He did not cry. He did not mourn. He did not care.

A few days later, he was released and sent to a new foster home. He ran away very quickly and went back to his father's house. Not long after, his father broke the news to him that he was moving the family back to Puerto Rico. He had finally saved up enough money from welfare fraud to buy plane tickets for the whole family and to build a house. Carlos decided not to go. At age sixteen, Carlos was completely alone. Overnight, he became homeless and had to learn how to survive on his own. There was no margin for error anymore. He started sleeping under the boardwalk and making money any way he could.

With no other option, Carlos learned how to live on the streets. He started with stealing bikes and anything of value he could find to resell. As he got older, he came up with more elaborate plots. The first technique he would use was quite complex. He would wait outside of bars and watch as couples parked and went in. At midnight, he would slash their tires. When they left to drive home, he would pretend he was walking by and noticed their tires were flat. He would offer to help patch up their tires if they gave him a couple of dollars. They would often be so tired or drunk that they would pay whatever he charged. Another of his schemes was to walk up and down the boardwalk all day with a Jerry Lewis Muscular Dystrophy Awareness can asking for donations, and then pocket the money. He didn't care about the cause; he only cared about buying drugs. If scamming people by making them think they were donating to a worthy cause allowed him to buy drugs, he had no qualms. Eventually, he started an underground business. People would tell him car parts they needed and as he walked up and down the streets of Ocean Grove, he would break into cars and steal the parts. He also learned to take advantage of his looks to stay by girls for the night. "I was evil," Carlos admitted.

When he turned eighteen and started to be tried as an adult, things got harder. His first adult sentence was eighteen months at the state penitentiary for burglary. Around this time, Carlos' crimes escalated from burglary to robberies. He traded his knife for a gun and as his income grew, his sentences increased in length. He got his first five-year sentence around this time. What surprised me was Carlos' attitude to prison. It really wasn't a punishment; Carlos saw prison as comfortable. Up until the early 2000s, corruption was rampant. Visitors would smuggle in drugs and the guards would be paid off. Carlos would be sheltered, fed, and still have the same access to drugs and alcohol that he had on the streets. When he got out of jail, he would go straight back to stealing and scamming. Carlos continued to rack up arrests to the point where he knew all the judges and police officers by name.

In Carlos's recounting, he skipped forward many decades to his final arrest. He and his cousin decided they wanted to do something big: they wanted to rob a bank. The night of their big plan, Carlos had a lot to drink to cool his nerves. On the train to meet his accomplices, he decided to rob someone. He pulled out his knife and took the man's backpack, phone, and wallet, then continued on his way. About an hour later, he was surrounded by the police and arrested for burglary. Thankfully, he hadn't reached his cousin yet to pick up his gun. Carlos was sentenced to ten years in prison with no possibility of an early release. For that entire period, he stayed alcohol and drug-free to avoid his sentence being extended. He was released in 2017, knowing that if he was ever convicted of another violent crime, he would likely spend the rest of his life in prison. He worked at a halfway house for a bit and then re-entered the world with a nice amount of money saved up and a debit card.

He stayed at a hotel for a few nights, quickly spent all his money on drugs, food, and clothes, and fell back to the streets. He started selling sheetrock and oregano as fake drugs and made enough money to stay afloat, but in that business, it is hard to get regular customers.

In the winter of 2019, Carlos nearly died. On winter nights that are below freezing, the Jersey Shore Medical Center allows people to spend the night. At 6 AM, the doors open for business and everyone leaves. One morning, after Carlos stayed the night, he felt so sick that he couldn't leave, so he asked for a medical checkup. While he was changing into the medical gown, he felt really dizzy, fell, and realized he couldn't breathe. He rushed out of the bathroom and passed out.

His body had shut down. Nine days later, he woke up from a coma. When he woke up he couldn't walk, eat, or use the bathroom. It took weeks in the hospital and over twenty months in a nursing home until he fully recovered.

When Carlos left the nursing home, he came to the Canright House. Like Larry, he realized his health was just not stable enough for him to survive on the streets. He needed to keep taking his medication if he wanted to stay healthy.

Throughout the entire interview, it seemed like Carlos was conflicted as to whether he should tell us the truth or tell us what he thought we wanted to hear. First, he told us that life in the Canright House is like life in prison for him. He tries to keep to himself and enjoy the luxuries of having a bed to sleep in, a shower every night, and three meals a day. Going to AA meetings and other events are the downsides, but a price he's willing to pay. Despite all of that, he mentioned that he'd come very close to relapsing over the last year, and if not for his relationship with his daughters and grandchildren, he would definitely be back on the streets.

Towards the end of the interview, he showed his institutionalized side. Carlos explained that once he gets his apartment he really wants to give back and volunteer at food pantries and the Center for Hispanic Affairs. He talked for five minutes about how he prays now more than he ever used to and even said, "I pray more because I got feelings today. I really got feelings. I don't like abuse. When I see someone here picking on someone else, that's the most degrading thing I hate."

Once we covered the majority of the content of Carlos' life story, I didn't try to push too hard for details. I had started to feel uncomfortable around him and wanted to finish the interview and get out. He kept touching my hand and even at one point took my folder and notebook to illustrate a point. For that reason, I skipped the assorted questions at the end and instead focused on a few more points he hadn't spoken about yet.

At one point in Carlos' life, he got married, had an apartment, worked an honest job, and had two daughters. An unspecified amount of time later, he had a huge fight with his wife while he was drunk, during which she said that he wasn't even their children's father. He got so angry that he started to beat her, and she ran to the other room and called the police. When he realized that she had called the police, he ran. Eventually, the police found and arrested him. He went to jail, got divorced, and lost touch with his daughters until after his final release from prison. Since then, he took a paternity test and confirmed that they are actually his biological daughters. Now, one lives in Englewood and the other in Tennessee, and he FaceTimes them and his four grandkids almost every day. I could tell by the way he talked about his kids that he was telling the honest truth; they are his biggest pride and his source of strength.

When asked if he had any regrets, Carlos skillfully avoided the question, but the next question tripped him up. When we asked about how he feels about his father now, his emotions got the better of him as he entered a rant which I will have to heavily PG-ify. Carlos understands that it was a different time, but doesn't forgive his father in the slightest. All Carlos ever wanted was attention and all he got was beatings. The last time he saw his father was when his daughter was three and he brought her to visit him in Puerto Rico. When she started to cry, his father told Carlos to take her away and he got really upset that his father wasn't showing her any love. They had a big fight and Carlos stormed out with his family. During his ten-year sentence, Carlos got the phone call that his father passed. He didn't even attend the funeral because he would have had to pay for a guard escort. He asked for pictures just to confirm he was dead and then ripped them up after. There was no love lost.

This next story makes me seriously doubt that Carlos has changed much over the last five decades. During our interview with James

Alai, we heard Manny screaming in the background about his carrots that someone had allegedly stolen. When we finished the interview, we rushed to the supermarket to buy carrots and then gave them to Manny. Carlos admitted to us that he had stolen and thrown out Manny's carrots because he wasn't doing his chores around the house, but when he heard what we did and saw the carrots in the refrigerator the next day, he decided to let them be. Then he ranted for a little while about how Manny needs to learn responsibility and that in prison, they teach lessons the hard way. It was clear to me his mindset is still that of a criminal and manipulator and that the only people who could really reach him are his children. I still have hope that Carlos will find satisfaction in life, but it will not be an easy journey for him and his supporters.

During the first alumni event, Carlos spoke, but we had not yet met him. In response to Dennis asking about what actionable steps he is taking in his life, Carlos explained that his goal is to learn how to empathize better with people. Due to his upbringing, his brain is wired to exploit others to accomplish his goals. Now he is trying to rewire himself to see the humanity in others. He talked about how his housemates each have their own struggles and are all striving for better, and how he is trying to see the world through the eyes of others as well as his own. Whether this is Carlos parroting what he has heard thousands of times before or him really trying to change his ways is very much up to interpretation.

11

The Press

This project had a lot of firsts for me: my first time raising money, my first time posting on Instagram, my first meetings with heads of organizations, my first time conducting a real interview, and my first time reading a news article about myself. Deion Johnson, from NJ.com, interviewed me and wrote an article about my efforts.

I was blown away the first time I read it. It took me almost three full read-throughs before it hit me that my efforts (and my face) were in the news. Only then was I actually able to absorb the content and appreciate the compliments that some of the people Johnson had interviewed had given me. One house member told Johnson that, "Zac looks at us as like a human being and not the way society deems us... if more people could be like him, it would be a better world." This compliment touched my heart because it articulated my biggest goal in this project—that we can see those less fortunate than us as human beings too and entitled to just as much respect as we are. That I had made him and others in the Canright House feel this was the best compliment I could ever receive.

After the article was released, my goFundMe page and winter clothing collections gathered significantly more attention. Just 36 hours after the article was released, we raised another $500 and dozens of people texted or called me about how to get involved.

Only a few weeks later, a second article was written about Project Unhoused in the Today Paper. Paul Petraccoro, the owner of the Today Paper, was so supportive of our efforts and even went as far as to highlight the article on the front page of the paper. This article also helped garner attention to Project Unhoused and the winter clothing drive.

After the article was published, Paul and I met at my house and he dropped off some clothes for the drive. We had a chance to converse and he was clearly such a kind-hearted soul with community service tattooed on his heart. I could tell that every issue he included in the paper was something he felt personally invested in. Paul put his full force behind the project and I am so grateful for all of his help.

12

Collection Stories

With the influx of donations to the winter clothing drive, my father and I offered to pick up the clothing from anyone who was somewhat far away. One Sunday, we spent almost three hours driving around Monmouth County picking up bags. Most of the people weren't home when we picked up the bags, but one woman came outside and we had a chance to get to know a little about our donors.

When we got to her house, I took the three bags off her porch and started walking to our car. Suddenly, though, the door opened and she introduced herself as Billie. She asked me a little about what I was doing and I explained Project Unhoused to her. Then she showed us what was inside each of the bags. One bag was filled with wool hats, gloves, and scarves she had knitted over the years, the other was filled with travel-size toiletries, and the last had tons of new socks. She had hit the nail on the head for the most needed items by those experiencing homelessness in the winter. Billie continued to explain how she is very involved with her church and that they've done drives like mine in the past. For those reasons, she knew which items were most vital and had put in extra effort to provide them. We ended up talking for almost fifteen minutes and exchanging phone numbers.

One of the other houses we visited that day had a card attached to the bag of clothing congratulating me on all my efforts. Almost all of the bags that had post-its with my name included a little smiley face or heart next to my name. It was clear that everyone who donated to the drive was so happy for the opportunity to help and appreciative of our efforts.

In synagogue the week after the article was released, many people approached me congratulating me and asking how they might help. It was extremely uplifting to feel the support of so many of my community members behind me. Even one of my teachers at school gave me a bag of old jackets. This feeling of support never ceased over the course of this project and I am so thankful for it.

13

Second Distribution

Only two weeks after our first distribution, we were amassing a huge pile of clothing in our garage. I reached out to Cherry, and we scheduled another distribution for the following Sunday. My father and I loaded all the bags into the car and were just barely able to fit everything. It took a while to get the trunk to close. Since it wasn't raining, we set up outdoors in a small empty parking lot on a corner lot. Cherry's son, Sahrue, brought two folding tables. We unpacked the car and got organized. Before we had even finished unloading, almost a dozen people had gathered.

For the next few hours, people streamed in at a steady rate. I didn't really understand where the people were coming from. Every couple of minutes another person would just walk over, seemingly out of nowhere. Later my dad pointed out that there were two motels nearby and a lot of people likely came from there, but he also felt that people would just round the corner and appear. It was a disorienting experience and highlighted just how invisible the problem could be. If I were just driving by, I never would have guessed so many people were homeless or in low-income housing and desperately in need of jackets, blankets, and pillows to make it through the winter. One Hispanic man introduced himself to my father and me and gave us his business card. He explained that he was a driver and asked us to share his information with anyone we could. He looked only a few years older than me, and I was extremely surprised when a few minutes later, his wife walked over holding an infant.

Once we had finished organizing everything and the foot traffic slowed down, Sahrue took out some beach chairs from his trunk and we sat down. Both he and his mother are incredible powerhouses of kindness in their communities. Sahrue gives out food to the homeless multiple times a week, and like his mother, is loved by everyone who walked by. Sahrue is a religious Moor and he explained that the central tenet of the Moor faith is loving and helping others and that this drives him to engage in charitable activities.

After two hours, almost everything had been given out. Cherry took the rest and gave it to someone at the motel whom she knows will continue to distribute it to those in need. This distribution was so rewarding and eye-opening; I never would have guessed we would be able to reach so many people so quickly. With the sheer amount of clothing we started with, I thought it would take hours to even make a dent in it. The magnitude of the need in Asbury Park blew me away and made me so grateful that I could help.

14

Meet Manny

Going into this interview, we already knew a little about Manny. James had told us that he is gay and flamboyant, and one of his closest friends in the house. Carlos told us that he is somewhat entitled and doesn't do his share of the chores around the house. When we met Manny, he was extremely personable and kind, but an hour later he was screaming at the top of his lungs about carrots. It was already clear he had two faces and that we would have to do a lot of reading between the lines.

By now we were accustomed to the operations of the house. Donna had warned us ahead of time that she wouldn't be there, so we asked Stacy to let Manny know we were there, then sat down and got started.

Manny was born in Philadelphia in 1970. He described his upbringing as good, on the surface. He had loving parents and grandparents, but his mother suffered from severe mental health issues which became more prevalent as he got older. His parents got divorced when he was five years old and he lived with his mother and three sisters. He remembers these years fondly. He has vivid memories of playing in his grandmother's candy store and the freedom of his early youth.

As he got older, his mother enrolled him in Catholic school, and by fifth grade, he was starting to struggle socially. He didn't do well with strict rules and didn't have many friends. He was already starting to figure out his sexuality and started to feel like everyone was against him. Manny said that the teachers supported the bullies and would curse at him and call him names. One day, he struck back, punched the teacher, and got expelled.

His mother was forced to put him in public school, and Manny was devastated. For the next few years, Manny didn't attend school. Instead, during the days he would sneak into museums by pretending to be part of a school's field trip and just read the exhibitions. There, Manny learned about the humanities and some of the sciences but never built a strong foundation in math. It took him five years to advance three grades, and eventually, his little sister caught up with him.

Manny realized that things were going very wrong, and decided to move to Cape May to live with his father and have a fresh start. He entered high school there as part of the special education track and started to actually enjoy school. He became very involved with the drama department in his school and performed the lead role in many of the musicals and plays. Things started to get awkward, however, when his father started dating his drama teacher and his school life became hard to distinguish from his home life.

Despite these complications, Manny was loving his new life in Cape May. He had average grades, made a lot of friends, and even became junior and later senior class president. Someone from the special education track being this successful was unheard of, but Manny was becoming a clear success story. He made it sound almost simple, saying, "I was driven, I wanted, so I went and I got it."

While all was well at school, Manny continued to struggle at home. All through this time Manny was coming to terms with his sexuality, and it didn't help that his father was extremely homophobic. Additionally, Manny started to prioritize his position in student council over his position as the lead in the school plays. His stepmother and all her friends put immense pressure on him to focus more on theater. Manny's relationship with his stepmother started to sour.

Going into senior year, an incredible opportunity presented itself. He heard of a statewide grant opportunity where one student would be given $300,000 to work on a social project. Manny came up with an idea way ahead of his time. He wanted to buy a trailer with trained doctors, psychiatrists, and therapists where kids could go to talk about their problems. There would be no records for visits and all patients would be anonymous. If a student had a problem with stress at home, mental health, addiction, sexuality, abuse, etc... they could go and seek professional help without bringing any attention to themselves. Manny got the grant and started the program immediately. It was a huge success.

While he was explaining the program to us, Manny let it slip that he had "a little drug problem" and kept hearing things would go on his permanent record, and that had been the major inspiration for the project. Then, he said, "Fast forward, I moved to New York." Immediately, I jumped in and asked when he had started using drugs. Only then did Manny reveal that throughout high school he had been using drugs very often. Once his addiction became public, he was ostracized and forced to leave Cape May. The program he founded cut ties with him, and he went to rehab. What Manny referred to as "a little drug problem" absolutely wrecked whatever trajectory he had in mind. He was stripped of all his accomplishments and became the paragon example of the destructive ability of drugs.

After going to rehab, Manny moved back in with his mother, went back to his old school, and graduated high school. Then, he went to Manhattan with twenty dollars and started a new phase in his life. When he got there, he met a gay man named Bob who took him in. Bob brought him down to Port Authority and showed him the complete poverty and homelessness there. Manny still remembers to this day what Bob told him: "These kids are throwaways. They are gay and their parents don't want or love them… Don't join them."

For the next year, Manny worked at a 50's era diner as a "soda jerk." He lived with three other struggling actors and made just enough money to stay afloat. One day, when he walked into work he met a girl, and "it was love at first sight." Less than nine hours later they were on a flight to Los Angeles. It wasn't until they were halfway across the country that he thought to ask how old she was—Natasha was seventeen, Manny was twenty. She hadn't even graduated high school yet. After two months on the West Coast, they flew back, Natasha finished high school, they saved up money, and then they moved to San Francisco.

At this point in the interview, I was quite confused. Manny was talking very quickly and giving us a lot of information with little elaboration. I felt uncomfortable to ask how he fell in love with a girl after being certain he was gay, but he didn't even hint towards it being any form of contradiction. I did ask if Natasha knew about his sexuality and he said they never had a real conversation about it, but she knew. Natasha's thoughts and her side of the story remain a mystery.

After about a year in California, Natasha and Manny moved back to New York. They both got very good jobs on Wall Street (Manny has no clue how). Manny stayed there for a few months but eventually moved on. Here, Manny and Natasha's paths diverged. Natasha continued to work at that company and climbed the ranks. Eventually, she went back to school to become a lawyer and now she has her own firm. Manny, on the other hand, went back to Philadelphia and moved in with his mother.

Manny's mother suffered from terrible mental health issues and frequently had frightening episodes. This period, when Manny was twenty-four, was the worst, and thankfully, the end of her nervous breakdowns. He shared just a few of these anecdotes which included his mother being dragged out of the house in a straitjacket and her breaking a broom over Manny's back trying to "get the devil out of him." The doctors told him to give up on her so that he would not be dragged down with her, but Manny beat the odds yet another time.

Back then, mental illnesses were not well understood. The doctors simply suggested she be admitted to a psychiatric ward. Manny got on the phone with her doctor and after over an hour of screaming and begging, he managed to completely reconstruct the doctor's view of mental illness. The doctor realized Manny was right, and found a way to treat Manny's mother. She ended up recovering, and the doctor continued to make regular phone calls to check in with his mother for the next ten years. In a later conversation, the doctor told Manny, "Your love for your mother and your understanding of this illness is a gift." Manny was so ahead of his time in his understanding of mental health and mental illness. He had two major successes in these areas, but both times drugs were his downfall.

Shortly after his mother recovered, his addiction got significantly worse. He jumped between Cape May and Philadelphia over the next few months without a stable place to stay. His father wouldn't take him in, and he was too proud to move back in with his mother, so he couch-hopped for most of the summer while working as a waiter. Around this time, Manny came out of the closet, and that was the final straw that severed his connection with his parents. His father wanted nothing to do with him.

It didn't take long for Manny to realize that he was practically a "throwaway kid." Bob had warned him over five years earlier, but he hadn't listened. Throughout his whole life, he had fought for his father's approval, but now he didn't care what his father thought about him. He was unshackled and unrestrained, and he felt he had descended to the lowest of the low. Over the next few years, he made the full descent to the same level as those boys in Port Authority. He got involved in all the debauchery that Bob had warned him about. As Manny put it, at age twenty-five, he got "eaten up by the gay community... the nightclubs, the drugs, the bathhouses, the bookstores, and the promiscuity."

Manny then fast-forwarded the story to years later when he had enough money to move from Philadelphia to Harrisburg, a suburban area with a large stable gay community. All I know about these years between moves is that when I asked him later about his first arrest, he mentioned that it was during this time period for prostitution.

In Harrisburg, Manny met Father Wallace, a Roman Catholic priest who was known to be extremely supportive of the Harrisburg LGBTQ community. Father Wallace served as Manny's impromptu dad and they grew very close. Things started to calm down. Father Wallace cosigned an apartment for Manny and helped him find a job in digital merchandising. Manny had finally found the life he wanted. He was ready to find a boyfriend, settle down, and live the way he wanted to without being judged.

Once again, drug use caused Manny's downfall. After another three years of balancing his addiction with his job, he tipped the balance too far. He lost his job, and his apartment, and went back to rehab. When he got out, he went back to the streets, got heavily addicted to crack, and lost himself. Manny completely transformed into an unrecognizable person. Over the next few years, he racked up significant debt, got kicked out of Harrisburg by the crack dealers there, lost his family house in Philadelphia, spent a lot of time in jail, contracted HIV, got involved with some really shady people, and continued using more powerful drugs.

In 2008, Manny hit rock bottom when two of his closest friends overdosed and died within a short time of each other. Manny was shattered and attempted suicide twice. Although he survived, he practically lost his will to live. He started using strong mind-altering drugs. During this time, he served two six-month prison sentences for drug use and had many manic episodes of drug-induced psychosis.

Psychosis is a mental health problem that causes people to have extremely realistic hallucinations and delusions (12). In one case, after using meth and bath salts, Manny had extreme paranoia which caused him to think the police were chasing and trying to kill him. Manny was walking along the street in broad daylight when a police car stopped and some officers got out to arrest him. The psychosis made Manny think they were a group of gay bashers, and his fight or flight instinct activated. He doesn't remember much after that aside from that his skull was crushed and the doctors put him in an induced coma for four days. He later learned that they had thought he was a purse snatcher and when he resisted arrest, it didn't help his case.

In 2014, Manny went through an intense rehab program, moved back to Cape May, and got a voucher for an apartment. He was finally independent again after all those years. He reconnected with his father and they started to mend their relationship. Unfortunately, it didn't take long for Manny to relapse. He went back to partying and doing drugs, but his situation was not nearly as dire as it had been in the past. He had an apartment of his own, had running water, three meals a day, and some leftover money to spend as he wished. As Manny put it, "I was functioning for the first time in my life. I was a functioning drug addict. I thought I had made it!"

In 2019, the narrative becomes very confusing. An old friend of his, Jane, came to visit and dropped off some meth as thanks for a favor Manny had done a while back. She brought Manny the meth, then had to go do something, but said she would come back the next day to hang out. Manny was then woken up in the middle of the night surrounded by police. It turns out that Jane had died from an asthma attack in the parking lot and the police thought he was associated. They searched his apartment and only found drug paraphernalia. He was charged for that, but things quieted down shortly after. A couple of months later, a guy

Manny had over for a date had a heart attack in his sleep and passed. Because of these two unrelated incidents, Manny was starting to look extremely suspicious to the police. A few months later, Manny was called into court for the two deaths. As a result of a complicated legal battle, Manny pleaded guilty to two counts of second-degree reckless manslaughter and served twenty-three months in prison.

This time was extremely transformative for Manny. It was the longest period he had been clean in many decades. This lucidity made him realize that he couldn't keep blaming others for his prison sentence because if he had not been using drugs, none of this would have happened. He started reflecting on his life and realized that every step of the way drugs had held him down. For most of his life, his brain had been wired to convince himself that drugs were bringing him overwhelming happiness when in reality they were pulling him away from everything he enjoyed and loved. From then on, Manny explained, "It wasn't horrible every day." He started to find joy in life.

When he was released from jail, someone told him about the Canright House since he is HIV-positive. As of our meeting, he had been here for six months. Manny has reconnected with his family and has been consistently attending meetings. Manny's perspective towards life now is one of true gratitude and appreciation. "Two people lost their lives so I can be here today," Manny said as his eyes started to well up with tears. "How can I ever not honor that? I've been given a totally new life." Manny hopes to become a peer support specialist so that he can help others who have made the same mistakes that he has.

Manny's interview took almost two hours on its own, so I didn't have a chance to ask many questions. Instead, here are some assorted stories from Manny's life that will help us understand his situation further.

Similar to how Carlos had some classic ploys that he used to make money on the streets, Manny had a process that he repeated over the years. Occasionally, Manny would find a man who was just starting to get addicted to drugs. He would make a deal with him whereby the man would continue to hold a stable job in the mornings, but once he came home, Manny would introduce him to the city's party scene and make sure he had a good time. In exchange for food and housing, Manny would ensure a constant supply of drugs while also acting as a stay-at-home dad, cleaning up the house, cooking meals, and running errands. In some cases, Manny would stay with someone for multiple years until they got too demanding or weren't making enough money to support two people.

For most of his life, Manny was couch-hopping. He didn't exactly have stable housing, but he very rarely was not able to find a place to stay. Between 2008 and 2010 though, Manny was literally homeless. On the streets of Philadelphia, Manny found a new community. He was taken in with open arms and taught all the particulars: where to hide his blanket and bedroll, which bathrooms he could use, where to get food, and how to get an address. He formed a partnership with a local Dunkin' Donuts whereby they would give everything they were going to throw out directly to him to distribute to the homeless. In exchange, Manny would ensure nobody would search through their dumpsters and make a mess. For the two years that Manny lived on the streets, he felt that there were plenty of resources and that there was a sense of camaraderie between those experiencing homelessness.

Whenever Manny was in jail, he had no access to drugs and was forced to go through a painful withdrawal. He explained that in more recent years, prisons have been easing that transition by giving inmates suboxone, a less powerful opioid. Manny explains that he thinks it is wrong that they make this detox process so easy. He has in mind a hardcore program that he thinks should be instituted in prisons where opiate users are given only what is absolutely necessary for them to survive. Instead of all the detox methods that are used now, he wants to make sure people don't starve or dehydrate and let their bodies take care of the rest. He believes that if inmates have to go through so much agony every time they go to prison, they might actually change their behavior. Then, after a halfway house program, he advocates for relocating them to the other side of the country where they don't know anyone and give them an opportunity to start a new life. This is similar to the program that Manny graduated from, and he believes it can help many others in the same position as he was in.

About an hour into the interview, we heard Carlos screaming at the top of his lungs. I don't know what it was about or whom it was directed against, but it was clear from Manny's reaction that these outbreaks were frequent.

At the end of the interview, we had a touching conversation in which Manny was talking about how it took him forty years to get back to where he started. When he was young, he genuinely cared about helping others. The trailer program he started in high school was his way of trying to help people experiencing the same struggles he had. Once he started using drugs, that portion of his brain just turned off. He was only able to think about himself. Now, he is finally reaching that emotional state again where he can find joy in helping others. With that being said, Manny gave me the most beautiful commendation for my efforts and said that when my father and I bought him carrots after James' interview, he was speechless. With that small action, we reignited some part of him that the drugs had blocked off.

15

Second Canright House Alumni Event

After our last interview, Donna let us know that they were having their second alumni event the following week. Before going to the Canright House, my father and I stopped by the local Dunkin' Donuts and picked up some more Munchkins. Cherry was working when we stopped by, and once again, she gave us discounted pricing for the Munchkins.

When we got to the Canright House, the event was already underway and Donna was speaking. We pulled up two folding chairs and sat in the doorway. The entire living room was decked out in Christmas lights with a large tree in the corner of the room. Stockings were hung along the walls behind the couch and Manny was beaming as we admired the decorations.

We missed the beginning of Donna's speech, but what we caught was very interesting. Donna shared with everyone an inspirational story about Carlos that he had been keeping secret. A few months ago, Carlos had met a homeless young single mother who was not receiving enough government aid to keep her and her child healthy. Carlos has been providing her with his extra food and money to keep them safe. It was such a rewarding thing to hear as in our interview, Carlos had appeared extremely callous. This story, and the fact that I heard it from Donna and not him, made me consider Carlos in a more positive light. While outwardly he doesn't seem to have changed much since he was a teenager, deep down inside, he clearly has a big heart and wants to help others.

Three alumni of the Canright House spoke, but none of them really elaborated too much on their stories. The message they gave was very similar to what we had heard at the previous event: everyone in the house is a family and should support each other through hard times. The most interesting portion was seeing this principle in action. Carlos shared that he had had an incredibly difficult week. Just the day before, he had come so close to relapsing and using drugs, but Larry was able to help him come to his senses. Only after an hour-long phone call with his daughter and a FaceTime with his grandchildren was he able to return to his status quo. If not for Larry keeping him accountable, he might have gone back to the streets.

This was concerning but reminded me that for everyone in that room, every single day was a fight. There is a construct in AA that a former addict is always an addict. You never quite shake the addiction, you just subdue it. All it takes is one bad decision to overturn a thousand good decisions. With that mindset, I was extremely proud of Carlos for being able to fight another day and escape unscathed.

Larry spoke after Carlos and shared that just two weeks ago he had quit smoking. This was a huge step in his life. While it hasn't been easy, Larry has been pushing through and taking actionable steps in his life. We all gave a round of applause.

James Alai shared that he is incredibly close to getting housing of his own. He estimated that it would only be a few more weeks before he would be able to move out of the Canright House. James also shared that he has absolutely no desire to do drugs anymore. He is ready to put his addiction behind him and reenter the world.

There was one point that Dennis, one of the alumni, made that really stuck with me. He stressed that if one really wants to change, they have to take actionable steps. Whether that is volunteering, decorating the house for the holidays, or thinking an extra two seconds before speaking—one has to do more than just skate by. The line of the night was, "Are you working to live or working to die?" It prompts the questions: Do you want to really change and come out of the House with a new life direction? Or do you just want to have a roof over your head and three meals a day until you die?

16

Local Politics

As we continued to collect more clothing, the small plastic bin in front of my house became practically useless. Every day after school I would come home and there would be at least three bags at the front door. Once it started to interfere with our Amazon deliveries, I started thinking about a more efficient system collection system. I talked to my parents, and they suggested I reach out to our local city council.

I wrote an email to the Ocean Township and Asbury Park City Council members about my efforts and asked about the possibility of having a collection location on municipal land. Additionally, I requested their help in advertising my winter clothing drive. Mayor Napolitani and I had a meeting scheduled less than an hour after I sent the email. Over the next two weeks, I met with Mayor Napolitani of Ocean Township and Councilwoman Yvonne Clayton of Asbury Park. These were the first two meetings that I attended alone and while I was very nervous going in, they both couldn't have gone better.

Mayor Napolitani was such a pleasure to work with. When I walked into his office, he had only a couple of decorations up. The largest and most proudly displayed was an award from the Affordable Housing

Alliance. It was clear from this and everything he said during our conversation that homelessness and pre-homelessness were very much on his mind. He introduced me to a couple of other people in the office and we scheduled a meeting where I could address the entire city council and petition my request.

I met with Councilwoman Yvonne Clayton, from the Asbury Park City Council, a week later and we had a productive meeting as well. We spoke about all the incredible nonprofits in the area, some of which I had already met with the heads of, and she provided the contact information for the organizations that I hadn't spoken to. We spoke about the Women's Hospitality Network, a coalition of churches that house homeless women one night at a time. I remembered that Billie Weise had told me about the organization and how she had wanted to conduct a women's products drive and donate it there, but she had not been able to contact the management. Councilwoman Clayton informed me that they had closed down during the pandemic. Despite her interest, Mrs. Clayton wasn't able to assist with my two requests and suggested I pair up with already existing organizations in Asbury Park.

A few days later, I met with New Jersey State Senator Vin Gopal, a champion of homelessness awareness and prevention. He runs an annual new sock drive for the homeless, participates in sleepouts, and just this year was instrumental in the passing of a bill securing $250,000 for youth homelessness prevention (13). We had a very fruitful meeting and the Senator introduced me to other organizations doing incredible work in Monmouth County. While we were talking, he mentioned that the Women's Hospitality Network had just reopened. I asked for the contact information of the founder, Stan Rosenthal, and forwarded it to Billie Weise along with the good news.

Overall, I was extremely impressed with the responsiveness of my local politicians. Every single Ocean Township councilperson responded to my email within three days, and once we met, they were so helpful in connecting me to organizations and giving advice.

17

Meet James Vick

J ames Vick was unlike any of the previous four men we had interviewed. While Larry, James Alai, Carlos, and Manny each had radically different upbringings, struggles, and dreams, they shared one thing that James Vick didn't have: a pure desire to share their story with me to help. James Vick had an ulterior motive which was clear as soon as we met him. Before our fourth interview, we finally were able to withdraw the funds we raised on goFundMe and distributed $50 Walmart gift cards as thanks to the people we had interviewed. No more than ten minutes after we gave out the cards, James Vick knocked on the door interrupting our interview with Manny to shake our hand and remind us that he was a resident of the house too.

During the interview, it was obvious James Vick was thoroughly institutionalized. Every question we asked got a direct response in as few words as possible and nothing more. He provided no details and incomplete stories. This wasn't the first time he was on the opposite side of a table being questioned and he gave us the same rehearsed answers that he was accustomed to giving. There was one moment where his apathy cracked just a bit and we saw a little deeper into his heart. With that being said, here is the story of James Vick, as he told it to us.

James was born out of wedlock in Newark, New Jersey in 1965, and lived with his mother and four siblings. His mother was a very strong woman who did what she needed to keep her children in line. His father was a bootlegger and later served in the army. He was somewhat involved in James' upbringing but took more of a part-time role. The detail he focused on is that when his father passed, he left James' mother with a lot of money.

After graduating from middle school, James went to an electrical wiring trade school but had little interest in education. The only insight he gave into this time period is that he was an avid basketball player. Up until he turned seventeen, James claimed he had never drunk alcohol or used drugs. But after the very first time he shot intravenously, he reached a high he had never experienced before and was hooked. James was very good at hiding his addiction from his family. His mother was starkly anti-alcohol and drugs, but for the next year and a half—until he graduated high school—James was able to keep his addiction under the radar.

As soon as James graduated high school, his life fell apart. It didn't seem like he cared that much though. He left home and started couch-hopping or sleeping on the streets when he couldn't find a place. He worked at a car wash for a little but would mostly panhandle or steal. All the money he accumulated went directly to fueling his drug addiction. After three years living on the streets of Newark, James moved to Asbury Park for a more quiet lifestyle. There he continued his life of homelessness, crime, and promiscuity. James gave us as few details as possible but mentioned the day he turned twenty-one he was tried for armed robbery as an adult and served five years in prison. My imagination was able to fill in the years between.

While he was in prison, James realized that he had contracted HIV presumably from a dirty needle. Over the next few decades, James' life followed a similar pattern. When he wasn't in jail, he would "run the streets" to make money. This might involve panhandling, petty theft, forceful robbery, or drug dealing. All the money he would make would go to buying drugs. Eventually, he would be arrested and sent back to prison. When he was released, the cycle would repeat.

Ten years ago, James had a five-year period where he stayed clean. He got an apartment through government programs, found a job, and was comfortable for the first time in decades. Unfortunately, one of the rules for his apartment was that no one else could live with him. When his girlfriend moved in with him, he got in trouble for violating the rule and lost the apartment. From there, he lost his job and fell back into homelessness. After a few more years on the streets, James was admitted to a nursing home after suffering multiple seizures. After nearly two years there, James left and moved into the Canright House. He has been here for the last two months.

Once James had gone through this information, I got the feeling he felt the interview should be over. His responses got shorter and more vague. His trademark phrase was "things of that nature" because it allowed him to avoid giving any specifics. Realizing I wasn't going to get the full story out of him if I didn't push, I started to ask more probing questions. The pressure yielded some interesting results.

James had skipped over a major detail in his childhood: he had a child at age fourteen whom he promptly abandoned. Over the years, he had four more children all born to different mothers out of wedlock. He called them every year on their birthday and Christmas but was mostly absent from their lives besides for the occasional fishing trip. He showed no remorse for the pain he put their mothers through.

Another interesting and unique aspect of James' story is that he never actually told his family he was homeless. He had too much pride to tell anyone because he knew they would help him, instead, he cut communication with his family. For all those decades, they did not know the pain he was going through. His mother lost her battle with cancer about five years ago and it devastated James. He didn't even know about her illness until it was too late. He acknowledged that this was the time he felt the most alone in his life. This was the only time James' poker face faltered and we recognized a hint of emotion in his voice. "I just wish the time would have been longer," James nearly whispered.

When asked about the camaraderie between those experiencing homelessness, James had only good things to say. He explained that most of the time, people helped each other; if someone didn't have a blanket, they would share. In the winter though, it was somewhat every man for himself. James said, "My animal instinct would take over. You just had to survive. Nobody bothers you, you don't bother them." He would always find a place to sleep either by the beach or in an abandoned building.

James is a very spiritual man. Religion has helped him through many hardships in his life including his mother's death. He finds comfort in knowing that God is watching over and protecting him. He attributes surviving overdoses on three occasions to God. He added that many of his close friends were not as lucky.

What surprised me the most was James' outlook on life: "You live and you die." James has had no goal throughout his life besides to make it another day. When I asked James what his happiest moment was he said "It is going to be waking up tomorrow." James' favorite things are being alive, being alone, and doing drugs. James' sole goal in life now is to live to 90, but my lingering question is what will his epitaph say? What is the legacy of a life just lived? It is my hope that before James turns 90 he is able to achieve something more than the motto tattooed onto his arm—"Let's live, laugh, and love."

Of all the people I had interviewed thus far, James left me feeling the most drained afterward. He treated our meeting as a chore, another annoying consequence of living. The $50 Walmart gift card was his sole motivation. I don't blame him for that. We are trying to get an unbiased sample and it is evident that living on the street for decades can make one callous and mercenary. In that world of favors and debts, there is no such thing as a free lunch. James is still in that mindset and seems unwilling to break out.

18

Third Distribution

Only two weeks after the previous distribution, the area my parents had allotted in our garage was overflowing. My father and I continued to drive around Monmouth County picking up bags of clothing. Almost every day when I came home from school, there would be two piles of bags on either side of our front door. I'd never received so many unknown texts and voicemails. Clearly, our project was gaining visibility.

On distribution day, we didn't even have enough room in our car for all the bags. Thankfully, my aunt, Ida Levy, came with a second car and took the dozen bags we couldn't fit. We arrived outside Cherry's project right on time, but she wasn't outside. We approached someone who was on their way in and asked if they could find Cherry for us. In the end, we had to wait for forty minutes before she came outside. Understandably, she was volunteering her time, but it wasn't uncommon for us to have communication problems with Cherry.

Once Cherry was ready, she directed us to a new location on the sidewalk in front of the Kingdom Komb barbershop. My father, aunt, cousin, and I unloaded the bags from the cars, opened up two folding tables, and got organized. My aunt made sure that we had the most organized setup yet. She was everyone's personal shopper and earned us a five-star customer satisfaction score.

Cherry had chosen this specific location because it was right next to the Asbury Park train station, a known gathering spot for those experiencing homelessness. Every twenty minutes, Cherry went over and told all the homeless men and women that we were giving out winter clothes. Each time she came back with six to eight people. It felt like a magic trick. Cherry even found a few whole families who we were able to help.

The atmosphere at the barbershop behind us was somewhat bleak as people didn't greet or acknowledge us on the way in and out. All the men and women who were there for the distribution were extremely friendly though. The Super Bowl was coming up the next Sunday and I had a very nice conversation with one man wearing an Eagles hat. There were a couple of young children who we were able to give stuffed animals.

This was the largest amount of clothing we had ever collected, but two hours later it was almost all gone. Once again, the magnitude of the need astonished me. Cherry just kept coming back with more people. After the seventh or eighth trip, I just couldn't believe there were still more people, but it never stopped. Everyone we met was so appreciative and kind. Afterward, I felt inspired and invigorated with purpose.

19

Lunch Break

I t would be hard to understand the context for the next few interviews without breaking the chronology a bit. Once summer started, I reconnected with Kevin McGee from Lunch Break, updated him on how the project was going, and thanked him for all of his help in the early stages.

As I've mentioned, the Winifred-Canright House is a shelter specifically for HIV-positive males. If we were to conduct all of our interviews there, we would hardly get an accurate sample. Since we had only interviewed men up to this point, Kevin offered to allow us to set up a table at Lunch Break while they supplied breakfast or lunch any day of the week. He knew of a couple of regulars who likely would be open to an interview and said he could introduce us to them.

During the months between our meetings, I had learned so much about homelessness and its psychological underpinnings, but in my conversation with Kevin, I realized that there is so much more to learn. He explained that adverse childhood experiences (ACEs) are a core factor in homelessness. These experiences are often severe like abuse, neglect, divorce, or loss of a parent. In addition to these ACEs, other factors can be extremely important in child development like nutrition, hygiene, how much stress the parents feel, and the safety of a home. These variables can affect a child from before they are born until they are seventeen (my age). Not only did he study this in college, but he had two decades of real-life experience.

This is exactly what the Family Promise division of Lunch Break is committed to assisting with. They provide food, clothes, shelter, transportation, and financial assistance to families experiencing homelessness. Not only do they cover the bare necessities, but they also teach the families valuable skills in budgeting, job applications and interviews, parenting, and household management. Their program is focused on keeping families together and equipping them with the skills to succeed long-term. Their 90% success rate shows they are extremely good at it.

After we spoke for about an hour, we scheduled our first interview through Lunch Break.

20

Meet Rose

The main Lunch Break facility in Red Bank was under construction, so in the meantime, they had been serving meals at a small lodge nearby. When we walked in, Kevin introduced us to the half a dozen men and women who were hanging out there before lunch. The room was pretty bare, with only a large television against one wall and a couple of folding tables that people were sitting at. Channel 4 News was on and everyone was watching the news or talking in small groups. Kevin introduced us to Rose who agreed to be interviewed.

Rose was born in Elizabeth, New Jersey, in 1943. Her father drank, but it never affected her much. Her parents were both extremely hard-working and worked to put food on the table and pay rent for their house. Rose went to Catholic school through high school and had no negative experiences. She was a shy and quiet child who kept to herself. Originally, Rose had wanted to attend nursing school, but her parents couldn't afford further schooling. Once she graduated high school, she began to work as a data operator at New Jersey Bell (now Verizon).

For the next twelve years, Rose lived with her parents and continued to work. At twenty-four she had a daughter out of wedlock. At twenty-nine, she moved in with her future husband, Richard, and they got married two years later. They rented in Keansburg, New Jersey, for a little while before moving to Fort Monmouth. There they bought a house and stayed for the next 31 years. She has worked at Humble Oil (now Exxon), Merck and Company, and Riverview Hospital each for significant periods of time. Richard worked as a carpenter and was in a union for a while but eventually started his own business. When Rose was fifty-four, Richard passed away from lung cancer. They were both smokers, though his death prompted Rose to quit shortly after.

When Rose turned sixty, she retired and started collecting social security. Rose and her son bought a house in West Virginia where he started a paving and seal coating business. Unfortunately, he didn't like West Virginia all that much and they moved back to New Jersey after two years. There they rented an apartment and Rose's son continued to work. Very slowly, they ran out of money. Their expenses simply outweighed their income.

The nail in the coffin was when their apartment had a bed bug infestation. Rose insists that it was not her fault, noting there had already been cases of bedbugs in the neighboring rooms. Regardless, the landlord tried to force them to pay for the exterminator. After Rose refused, they lost the apartment, and her credit was destroyed. Rose and her son moved into a motel in a bad area where they stayed for the next four and a half years. The room had bugs and mold, but at least it was a roof over their heads. Rose mostly kept to herself and avoided interactions with the neighbors for her own safety. All through this time her son continued to work and she collected social security, but it wasn't enough to support them, and eventually, they couldn't afford to pay the rent.

Just last year, Rose and her son became homeless. She lived in her truck for three months before she joined the Women's Hospitality Network for the winter. She had a place to sleep and would go to various places for meals and entertainment. During these months, Rose had one incident where her truck broke down and needed repairs and she couldn't get around. While her car was being fixed, the Jersey Shore Adult Day Care took care of her. She had such good things to say about the existing organizations in Monmouth County in every category aside from housing. Once March came around, the program ended and she went back to living in her truck. At the beginning of July, she had found temporary housing at a shelter, but on September 1st, her stay expired and she had nowhere to go.

Rose is in touch with social services but unfortunately, they can't do anything to help her. They have three programs and she doesn't fit into any of them. She collects social security and food stamps which give her enough money to survive, but she doesn't have a place to stay. Since she was evicted twice, she cannot find an apartment. She was given lists of organizations and churches to reach out to but has had no luck finding a place to stay. As of now, she plans to move back into her truck two weeks after the writing of this chapter.

Rose and her daughter are no longer in contact. Her daughter is now fifty-six, and last they spoke she was living in Ohio. Rose explained that her daughter has bipolar disorder, but doesn't take her medicine and that she has been through nine marriages. Rose's son is now forty-nine years old and is living on the streets and working when he can. He has two children ages twenty-seven and sixteen for whom he pays child support. Rose gives him food stamps when he needs and their bond is unbreakable. Through all sorts of hardships they've stuck together and he continues to love and care for her in any way possible.

Rose's life story was absolutely heartbreaking. After working for over forty years, buying a house, and raising and supporting two children, she retired and hoped to finally relax. But as a senior citizen, society failed her. Now eighty years old, Rose is soon to be homeless again. I just don't understand how that can happen, nor can I accept it. As she went through her life, I was waiting for the big moment when everything fell apart, but it never came. Rose experienced an extremely slow descent into poverty and homelessness and was unable to point to one specific cause. I continued to dig deeper asking if either Rose or her son had any problems with addiction, but besides for smoking, there was nothing huge. Rose gambles and drinks a little, but it was never a problem. Rose could not point to any decision or mistake that caused them to run out of money, it just happened.

What was equally surprising was Rose's outlook on her life. Rose is one of the most optimistic and positive people I know. Despite such adversity and pain, she sees the world through happy-tinted glasses. There was not an ounce of negativity in our hour-long conversation. Rose made many statements that made sense logically, but in practice, required supreme control over her emotions. She said, "What am I going to do by being mopey? It's not going to solve anything, and I'd rather be friendly with people and have a smile on my face." Rose's biggest piece of advice was to "roll with the punches." Things will happen, but you can always overcome them with a smile. Rose lives with a mentality of not dwelling on the past, but finding enjoyment in the present.

21

Fourth Distribution

For the month after the previous distribution, we struggled to reach Cherry. Since she wasn't answering calls or texts, we called her son, Sahrue. He informed us that she had lost her phone and was getting a new one soon. In the meantime, he said, we should text him in order to reach her. He would not respond to texts, however, and the first few times we called him, he failed to relay the message to his mother. It took a while, but eventually, we were able to schedule a distribution.

During the month-long period we had not been able to contact Cherry, the clothes had piled up to an all-time maximum in our garage. This was going to be our biggest distribution yet. When the day came, my uncle brought his car as well and it took almost twenty minutes to pack both of the cars. When we got to Cherry's project she shared with us the unfortunate news that Sahrue had not been able to join us, so we had to cram her and two tables into our cars as well. She squeezed into the back seat of our car while we put the two tables in my uncle's Jeep. They were somewhat hanging out the back window, but they survived the drive.

We set up in the same parking lot as our second distribution. The major difference this time was that after an hour and many dozens of people, we still had not given away half of the clothes. Over the next hour, we continued to make slow progress and meet a lot of very nice people, but as it got later in the day, things began to quiet down. During the distribution, we saw someone we recognized. Mark Wilson used to be my great uncle's employee in the 80's and slowly became a central part of our family. He is my cousin's godfather and I've known him forever. He happened to be walking through Asbury Park and spotted us. He shared so many memories about the area, like how the apartment he grew up in was down the block, and that he used to work in the building whose parking lot we were in. He ended up staying and helping us for half an hour.

A little after Mark left, we had a bit of an incident. To set the scene, my father and I wear yarmulkes and are easily identifiable as Orthodox Jews. My father, Cherry, and I were standing on one side of the table organizing items and helping two very nice older men. A younger man walked over to Cherry and asked her a question very loudly, "Do you read the Bible?"

"I am a Muslim so I read the Bible and the Quran," Cherry replied.

"Did you know," he interrupted, "that on the way to Mecca, Muhammad forced people to convert by the sword." His rude comment took us all by surprise and no one said a word. All of us just turned toward him and stared as he continued to slander the Quran and the Bible. I was clueless as to how to respond.

"Where are you from?" he asked my father and me.

"New Jersey," my dad responded.

"No, like where are you actually from?" My father paused, unsure how to answer, and the man angrily flung a flurry of words at us of which I only caught "You come from pigs."

"We are all the sons of God," my father responded, trying to defuse the situation.

"No, we are not," he spit back.

"What do you believe in?"

"I believe I am a true Israelite and that we are at the end of days. Very soon we will be asked to take up arms and I will be a soldier for God..." He rambled on.

"Can we stand beside you?" My father interrupted.

"No, you will serve us. Because you enslaved us we will enslave you."

My father stopped engaging with him. No one said a word. I wanted to push for an explanation but knew I shouldn't. We all just looked at him with empty smiles.

He continued, "You are smiling because you know it's true. You may have the money and power now but soon you are going to be our slaves."

One of the older men said, "The Bible also says to respect your parents and elders. You are just too young and don't have the knowledge to understand..."

He interrupted, "How old was Solomon when he became king?" He realized he wasn't getting through to anyone and walked away.

When he was out of earshot Cherry said, "Some people are crazy. All we can do is pray for him." A few minutes later one of the older men pulled me aside and advised me, "When you do good the devil will try to stop you. Don't let people like that put you down."

We cleaned up shortly after, gave all the leftover clothes to the man at the motel nearby, and drove Cherry home. I was very spooked and my father and I unpacked various factors. Were we putting ourselves into a dangerous situation? In the end, it was a scary and upsetting experience, but it could have gone worse. The man had not presented any physical danger and had left pretty quickly. Overall, the hate from this man was overshadowed by all of the good interactions and kind people I met that day.

22

More Press

As time went on, many more articles were written about Project Unhoused and I grew more comfortable in interviews.

The next article to be written was in a children's magazine called AIM. Dina found my Instagram and reached out to see if I would be interested in being featured in the "Kids Who Give" section of their magazine. I was honored! She sent me a list of questions which I answered, and a few weeks later, she sent me a draft of the article. It was so exciting to know that my efforts were being used as inspiration and education for young kids. A few weeks later, Saskia, who operates an Instagram account named Happy Headlines, also approached me regarding Project Unhoused. She sent me a list of questions and only a few days after I responded, she posted an incredibly well-written article about the project. Both Dina and Saskia were such a pleasure to work with and very supportive of Project Unhoused.

Around the same time as these articles, William Clark from *The Coaster* reached out to me about writing an article. We spoke on the phone and got along really well. He asked me some questions about the project, and before he hung up, he gave me a very nice compliment. He said that he was incredibly impressed with all of the work I've done with Project Unhoused, but even more than that, he was blown away by how I held myself in an interview. This was extremely rewarding as it was the last media interview I've had to date. It meant that the progress I had felt over the last year when it came to meetings and interviews was not just imagined, it was noticed. This was a huge milestone and a confidence boost for me. Only a few weeks after our call, the next edition of *The Coaster* was published with Mr. Clark's article.

Here, I would like to acknowledge a huge supporter of mine from the beginning of Project Unhoused: Eileen Mizrahi. Eileen is my grandmother's very close friend and an incredibly kind woman. When I first told her about the project and the winter clothing drive, she told me, "Spending so much time in Manhattan, I always wanted to help the homeless, but didn't know how. Thank you for giving us this avenue!" A few weeks later, she dropped off bags of coats and blankets. After the article in *The Coaster* was published, Eileen came to my house and gave me a laminated version of the article and the most beautiful letter. Thank you Eileen for your continued support!

23

Meet Ellen

For our next interview, Kevin introduced us to a woman at Lunch Break's clothing bank, Clara's Closet. There wasn't an ideal spot for us to sit down to talk, so she sat on the stairs as my father and I set up two chairs. We were obstructing the door and eventually found a better place in a tight hallway. For her own safety, she asked if we could avoid using her name in the book, so going forward I will refer to her as Ellen.

As soon as we met Ellen, it was clear she suffered from excruciating back pain. She wasn't able to stand straight and her walk was more like a shuffle. Aside from her posture, Ellen looked like a typical middle-aged white woman. In fact, fifteen years ago, she had been. Out of privacy, she preferred not to talk about her early life. Ellen started her story in 2012 when Superstorm Sandy struck New Jersey. For the years before that, Ellen had been working hard and was barely scraping by. She had an apartment she was content with and a little savings. While things weren't exactly prosperous, Ellen was able to pay rent, put food on the table, and help her friends and community members. She was independent and in charge of her life. Retrospectively, Ellen recognized that her cost of living was going up faster than her wages.

She was trapped in a slow death spiral with or without Superstorm Sandy.

Nonetheless, Superstorm Sandy accelerated the process. The first few days of the storm weren't terrible. The electricity and gas went out, but everyone was optimistic that things would return to normal. Ellen had prepared in advance by filling her freezer to the brim with ice. Since she was on a higher floor of an apartment building, the flooding affected her a lot, but not nearly as much as it affected the lower floors. By the third or fourth day without power, she heard that a friend had gas. She figured that rather than let all the meat in her freezer go to waste, they could cook it together. She opened the freezer to get the meat and gallons of cold water poured straight onto her. She lay down on the floor and cried.

Over the next week, things only got worse. Being so close to the ocean, the storm surge had a huge impact on her community. In a storm of that magnitude, the ocean rises way above normal sea level before returning to the ocean as the storm passes by. The water doesn't come back the same way it leaves though. Ellen explained that the storm surge dragged back all sorts of dangerous chemicals and bacteria from paints, pesticides, natural gas, and sewage. This water is often toxic and can leave houses and apartments nearby uninhabitable. Almost all of Ellen's neighbors' apartments were infested by toxic mold, and she started getting really sick from all the exposure. She lost over thirty pounds and had no energy.

Regardless of how bad the situation was, Ellen did not give up. She drove to every single relief agency and filled out hundreds of forms. In retrospect, though, Ellen called it all "a waste of time." FEMA brought in over 7,500 staff to help, but in Ellen's experience, they did nothing besides fill up hotel rooms with their staff (14). Ellen said that what happens in the wake of a disaster is that "you are on your own."

In total, electricity remained inaccessible for two weeks and gas for

91

two and a half months. Ellen visited every single organization within driving distance but no one could help her find a new place to stay. She was surrounded by toxic mold but had no other option besides sleeping on the streets. She felt so vulnerable. Having heard that a nearby apartment had burned down due to a gas main blow, Ellen was absolutely terrified about what the coming months would hold. Superstorm Sandy hit in the winter, and she knew that once the weather warmed up, the toxic mold would grow exponentially worse. When the holidays came around she didn't have enough food to celebrate. Thankfully, a nearby restaurant, the Langosta Lounge, was hosting a holiday dinner for the community. Ellen spent her holiday there, but it only reminded her of how far she had fallen. In recollecting this, Ellen started crying as a rush of emotions returned. Only a few months earlier, she had been the one helping others. Now, there she was; all of her Christmas decorations had been lost in the flood and she was accepting charity on Christmas. Ellen couldn't look anyone in the eye. She felt that she no longer had any control over her life. Everything had been ripped away and she was forced to be dependent on others.

Without the help of community organizations, Ellen would not have made it. The food and clothes they provided made it possible for her to survive the disaster. Still, the main problem was housing. She was only ever able to find one apartment for rent, but it was unaffordable (double the price of her old apartment), much smaller, and located in a dangerous area. Hotel and motel prices had doubled as well and she just couldn't afford to live anywhere else. Thankfully, Ellen got very lucky and didn't have to move onto the streets. A friend of hers allowed Ellen to move in with her. After a few months, Sandy had become old news and the world moved on. There was no long-term aid.

For the last twelve years, Ellen has been couch-hopping or living on the streets. Her health has progressively gotten worse and her luck finding housing has taken a similar trajectory. At almost every agency

Ellen applied to, she was informed that she wasn't eligible because she wasn't over sixty-five, wasn't Hispanic, and didn't have children. Some organizations had different criteria, but Ellen never quite fit the bill. She expressed her anger at how many programs are rehabs that offer housing afterward, but ironically, since Ellen has never touched drugs, that avenue is closed to her. Even if she had managed to get approved for affordable housing, Ellen heard that in some cases the wait time is over three years.

Ellen recently turned sixty-five and is now eligible for different benefits. She finally has Medicare and can now be treated for her severe health problems. Still, she cannot afford special procedures, like an MRI, or dental care. The housing situation for seniors is just as flawed. They all charge a fee, upwards of $45, each time someone applies for housing. This would be reasonable as a one-time fee for gathering information which would be stored in a database for all other organizations, but in reality, the applicant must pay it again for every single program they apply to. Ellen is convinced this is nothing more than a money-making ploy.

Ellen opted not to reveal where she was staying, simply conceding that she had a place to sleep. She is unable to work because of her back problems. I have no idea what the future holds for her, but I am confident she can overcome any challenge that stands in her way despite the fact that the system is deeply flawed.

In this interview, Ellen introduced a lot of ideas and problems that I hadn't heard about before. In this section, I will explore those topics and add what I learned in my research after the interview.

For starters, I had never fully considered the impacts of natural disasters to the extent Ellen revealed to us. I was five years old when Superstorm Sandy hit. All I remember is that we stayed by my grandmother's house for a few days after a tree fell and nicked our house. It was raining a lot and there were strong winds, but we were safe from it all. After the power was restored, everything returned to normal. Although the five-year-old me didn't know it, Superstorm Sandy was the most devastating natural disaster in New Jersey history. There were over 346,000 homes destroyed and $30 billion dollars in damages (15). For years after the storm hit the aftermath could still be seen and felt.

Given that I never had experienced the devastation that natural disasters present, I hadn't fully considered them as a major cause of homelessness. In all of the conversations I'd had to date, natural disasters had never come up. After speaking with Ellen, it seems like such an obvious correlation. It is extremely difficult for anyone close to the brink of homelessness who is affected by a natural disaster to keep their job and housing. Suddenly they are unable to work and have a lot of extra expenses. If they can't tread water until they get insurance money, then their lives can fall apart. Additionally, many of the local aid organizations like shelters and food banks were flooded and destroyed in the storm itself. People are truly left to fend for themselves.

In response to Superstorm Sandy, the government provided over $50 billion for emergency relief to the 24 states affected (16). I searched online and besides from the $15 billion allotted to New York City, I struggled to find exactly where that money went. Online it says that the Federal Emergency Management Agency (FEMA) was the first to respond and spent $10 billion flying in medical personnel and giving food, water, and medical supplies to those in need. The numbers they report are staggering: they flew in over 7,000 personnel and provided millions of water bottles, hundreds of thousands of meals, and over $600 million directly to those in need. In Ellen's experience on the ground, however, FEMA was a waste of time. She spoke at length about her frustrations with the agency. She felt that all the personnel they flew in caused more harm than benefit as they further inflated the unaffordable hotel prices. Ellen also felt that their numbers were extremely overblown and they cared more about receiving applications than actually fulfilling them. As a result of these deficiencies, Ellen and thousands of others fell through the cracks.

Ellen's advice for anyone who might be facing a similar situation is simple: leave! According to US News and World Report, New Jersey has the fourth highest cost of living of all the states (17). As soon as disaster hits, Ellen suggests going to a state with a lower cost of living. Housing is cheaper, taxes are cheaper, and a dollar goes further. For many social services, the amount of money you are given is not calculated based on where you live. Since the cost of living is so high in New Jersey, the money given is just not enough to survive on. The federal poverty level for an individual is $14,580 a year (18). Meanwhile, the minimum an individual needs to earn in order to get by in New Jersey is $38,910 (19). Over two million people in New Jersey make too much to qualify for federal support, but not enough to survive without aid (20). For this reason, Ellen explained that those experiencing homelessness are incentivized not to work. The higher their wages are, the fewer benefits they receive, and eventually they get stranded in this no man's land between the federal and state poverty levels. Until this problem is resolved by legislation scaling government assistance to the cost of living of the state, Ellen suggests others leave New Jersey and move to states where life is cheaper.

Ellen got very emotional as she was telling us about how it feels psychologically to be homeless. The change in her economic circum-stances forced her to become a taker rather than a giver. Originally, she couldn't face those who were helping. It reminded her of all that she had lost and how far she had fallen. Ellen also suffers from serious PTSD surrounding the storm. For the first few weeks, she was extremely afraid for her life. She was hearing reports of fires and chemicals while she was slowly feeling sicker because of the toxic mold in her apartment. With what little energy remained, she drove to anywhere she thought she could get help. Ellen became extremely depressed as every single organization turned her down. Without health insurance, she has been unable to receive any counseling for this trauma.

Since becoming homeless, Ellen has been insulted at length for being unhygienic. Her response is that she doesn't want to be dirty, but she doesn't have a choice. It is not easy to get access to a shower and it is even harder to find one with warm water. "Everybody sweats," Ellen said, but she doesn't have deodorant or a change of clothes at the end of the day.

In the last few years, Ellen has been able to reclaim some form of giving back. With so much experience living on the streets, she has been able to help those who recently became homeless by connecting them with organizations. When people land in crisis, they need to find help as soon as possible, and there is no easy way to learn about all the resources available and what you may qualify for. Ellen has been able to help many people experiencing homelessness for the first time in this manner. One of Ellen's major recommendations was that more umbrella/one-stop-shop organizations (like Lunch Break) be formed. This would remove redundancy and make it significantly easier for everyone to get the help they need. Additionally, it would remove the problem of duplicate application fees.

While we were talking, the topic of motels came up and Ellen had some really interesting things to add. Ellen explained that staying in a motel is considered being homeless. Motels are merely a stopgap and once one reaches that stage, there is little hope to avoid experiencing homelessness. Living in a motel, they can't amass possessions. They have to be light on their feet and be ready to leave on a moment's notice. What was even more disturbing is how expensive motels can be in Red Bank—$150 a night. That is an absurd price given the stories I've heard about these motels and their revolting conditions. It is simply unsustainable.

Of all the topics we discussed, Ellen made it clear that one is the most important. She said that the majority of homelessness cases are not caused by drug and alcohol addictions or mental health problems. Ellen said that the main reason people become homeless is the lack of affordable housing. Ellen had enough savings to last for a few weeks, but without a safe place to live, she wasn't able to get back on her feet. If one of the relief organizations had been able to supply her with a hotel room until they could remove the toxic mold from her apartment, she would have been able to continue to work and support herself. This is shocking and seems to be a relatively simple problem to solve.

24

Council Meeting

After my meeting with Mayor Napolitani, I scheduled a meeting with the entire Ocean Township City Council to discuss Project Unhoused, request municipal drop-off locations for my winter clothing drive, and ask if they could help advertise my efforts. I wish I could say I wasn't nervous going in. I had grown very comfortable with individual meetings, but the idea of talking to that many people in an unknown environment was still overwhelming. When we drove over to the municipal building and I actually saw the room, my anxieties subsided. The city council members were seated around an oval table and I had already met most of the people in the room individually.

As soon as they were ready for me, I told them about Project Unhoused and asked for their advice and assistance. Instantly, the room turned into a brain trust. The atmosphere loosened and everyone just started coming up with ideas. Councilman Acerra had an idea on how to collect reusable bags. Councilwoman Kelly came up with a plan to collect toiletries. It was an extremely collaborative environment. The entire council was so supportive of my initiative and said it would be "no big deal" to designate the collection facilities and advertise them.

Mayor Napolitani put me in touch with the Public Works Department to move forward on those projects.

After the council accepted our request to collect winter clothing in municipal buildings, I met with Mark Disakias and Tracey Berkowitz to discuss the specifics. We had a very productive meeting in which they offered to lend us four recycling bins which we could decorate and put in the town hall, municipal gym, human services department, and library. Tracey and Mark recommended that we run three one-month-long drives in November, January, and April. Since they were only able to approve a winter clothing collection, at the end of the meeting we left it that I would design the bins and we would reconvene to install the bins before October. Additionally, Tracey suggested we collect clothing at various Ocean Township events and introduced us to Jen Nordstrom who runs Fall Fest.

Since then, Jennifer and Danny Aboudi from Monmouth County Speedpro Imaging generously produced and donated us boards to decorate the recycling bins. We plan to collect during the Fall Fest this upcoming September and to install the recycling bins in the municipal buildings come October. This will allow us to reach significantly more people in our collections and help so many more of our neighbors who are on the brink of or experiencing homelessness.

25

Fifth Distribution

When it came time to schedule the next distribution, we reached out to Cherry using the new phone number she gave us but got no answer. This was unsurprising as Cherry had always been difficult to contact, but after calling and texting her four times in two weeks with no response, we started to get worried. We drove to the Dunkin' Donuts where Cherry works, but the staff told us she had been fired.

Unsure how to proceed, we continued to call and text until Sahrue finally answered another two weeks later. He did not give us any details on how Cherry was faring, which was our largest concern, but told us that we could have a distribution in two Sundays and that he would pass the news on to his mother. It was settled. We had a crazy amount of donations and my friend, Joseph Aboudi, offered to help drive his dad's work van and help us with the distribution. When we sent a text confirmation to Cherry and Sahrue a few days before, we got no response.

When Sunday finally came around and they still hadn't responded, we had no idea what to do. Should we call off the distribution or pack the bags possibly for naught? Instead, we came up with a plan, my father and I drove to Cherry's project without loading the car. If she was ready, we would call Joseph, go back home, pack the car and van, and come back. When we got to her housing project, Cherry was nowhere to be seen. We found someone outside who knew her and asked if they might go upstairs to check her apartment. After we were waiting outside for ten minutes, they told us Cherry wasn't home. I called Joseph and we went back home. We continued to call and text Cherry and Sahrue over the next week, but none of them ever responded.

Now we had a problem on our hands. We had a garage full of winter clothing, but no way to safely distribute it to those in need. We briefly considered running a distribution on our own, but given the antisemitic episode we experienced at our last distribution, that idea was quickly dismissed. After a week of mulling over the problem, I had the idea to reach out to Mark Wilson, a close friend of my family who we had seen and caught up with at the last distribution, to ask if he would be able to help. To our delight, he was beyond excited! He immediately jumped into action and put his full weight behind Project Unhoused. We planned a distribution for the next Sunday and it turned out to be our biggest success yet!

We had our largest supply yet as it had been over two months since we'd had a distribution. Thankfully, Joseph Aboudi was available to help again. He brought his dad's work van and together we were able to fit all of the bags and three tables. We drove over to the parking lot, met up with Mark, and started to set up.

Over the next few hours, people streamed in. There were quite a few familiar faces and tons of smiles. Mark had the biggest smile of everyone though. He was so glad to be able to help and although it was sad that Cherry wasn't by our side, I felt like Mark gained so much joy from the experience. Mark knew just about everyone who passed by, and I'd estimate that every tenth car rolled down the windows to greet Mark. One of Mark's friends even pulled over and joined us for a while.

Remember the Hispanic family I had met during the second distribution? The father had explained to us that he was a driver and had given us his business card. It warmed my heart to see his wife pick up some English early-reading books for her daughter and place them in their bag. Without a doubt, this was the highlight of the distribution. First of all, I was able to speak to them in Spanish to help them find what they were looking for. Secondly, I could picture the long-term benefits of having books like that in the house. They are clearly extremely hard-working parents trying to give their kids a better chance than they had. In a small way, I was able to help.

While we were helping a few people, I noticed that there was a man across the street who didn't look well. He was wearing worn-in Timberland boots with the laces undone and no socks underneath. His shorts were tattered and his shirt had tons of rips and strings hanging off. He kept shifting his weight from foot to foot and making little hops while his hands tugged at the ripped parts of his shirt. Eventually, he hobbled over to our side of the street without even checking for cars. Joseph went over and offered him a water bottle. He asked for two.

While Joseph went to get him a drink, he came up to my father and me and started reciting a memorized sob story. It was like he was reading off a script. I don't even remember the details. He put no emotion into the words and it was clear he was high. Meanwhile, one of the women who we were helping at the time came over and dragged him aside. It turns out they were cousins and she was really upset. She told him to leave and stop embarrassing himself, but he was clearly not thinking straight. He didn't say a single coherent thing, rather, he just started screaming. Thankfully, Mark got involved and broke up the argument. What I gathered from their screaming was that the man had missed an important family funeral and had been living on the street for a while while using drugs.

After Mark broke up the argument, the man stumbled back across the street and left. The girl regained her composure and apologized to us for the fighting. It was a hard encounter to witness, but it was the first time I was able to see the effects of drug use in action. The man had lost the ability to comprehend logic. He was in his own world, and I couldn't change that. All we could do was give him a drink and offer him some new clothes while praying that he finds the strength to overcome his addiction.

After a few hours, we had given away most of the clothes and it was getting late. We gave the remaining items to the same place as before and packed the tables into the van.

26

Meet Ruth

After our meeting with Rose, she suggested that another one of her friends might be interested in being interviewed. When we came back to the lodge the next week, Rose's friend and her daughter were there. She preferred for her name to be omitted from the book, so I will be referring to her as Ruth.

At eleven years old, Ruth ran away from home. Both of her parents were extremely abusive physically and sexually. Her mother used to say, "You have to get your experience somewhere, might as well be from your father." After Ruth escaped, she started living on the streets and working at a diner while attending school. One day, the owner of the store picked her up from school and brought her to a hotel along with some coworkers and friends. He told her, "Do what I say or you get fired from your job." Ruth was continually sexually abused until she was fourteen. For all of those years, she lived in a state of fear with absolutely no protection. I could see in her eyes that past her tears a tinge of fear was awakened as she revisited the horrific memories from her childhood. I couldn't help but tear up as well.

One day at work, Ruth met a Greek man who offered to take her in. She had been abused by so many before, but she saw something in him that she trusted. Thank God she was right. He gave her a separate room and took good care of her. Ruth was finally safe. She found a new job at a restaurant where she was treated with respect. She put her family behind her and found some form of joy in living.

After they had been living together for a few years, Ruth "made the first move" and their relationship became more intimate. Despite the age difference, they eventually got married and when Ruth was twenty-one, had a daughter. Ruth continued to work at the restaurant while her husband worked in construction. Their daughter had some developmental delays and it was very difficult for Ruth and her husband to balance all the doctor's appointments and their careers. Most of the burden of care fell upon Ruth as her husband wasn't fluent in English, but Ruth couldn't drive. As a result, Ruth regularly missed or canceled appointments, and the doctors called child services on her. Ruth had to fight hard to keep her daughter, but she prevailed and still today her daughter is right by her side. Four years later, Ruth had another daughter who had similar developmental delays. She had to quit her job to take care of the two of them, but she loved her daughters more than anything else and was willing to give the world to them. A few years later, after a miscarriage, they had one more daughter together who sadly passed away at four months old.

Through this time, despite all the challenges, Ruth's life was stable. Her husband made enough money to support their family and she took care of her two daughters. When she was thirty-eight, Ruth started taking care of an older man in her community who was all alone. He had a son who lived in Ohio and was eagerly waiting for his father to die to collect his estate. Ruth became his caretaker and he grew extremely close with their family. At one point, Ruth's family moved in with him and started paying rent. He taught Ruth to drive, sent her to college, and gave Ruth's husband a job in real estate. He was the father Ruth never had, the grandfather to Ruth's children and the entire family's guardian angel. In 2017, Ruth's mother-in-law fell ill and her husband went back to Greece to take care of her.

Around this time, the older man started having severe heart problems and the doctors recommended he have open-heart surgery. His son refused to fly in to help and even tried to cancel the surgery altogether. Ruth, behind the son's back, scheduled the surgery and stayed by the older man's side throughout the entire fifteen-hour process. When she called the son afterward to say the surgery was successful, he was audibly upset.

In 2020, the older man needed to have a follow-up heart surgery and although it was a success, afterward, he took a turn for the worse. While he was on his deathbed, the hospital called his son and all he responded was, "Call me back when he's gone and give me the time of death." Ruth was by the older man's bedside when he passed overnight.

When Ruth woke up, the son had already received the phone call and jumped into action to get his revenge. The son blamed Ruth for prolonging his father's life. His complete callousness and disregard for his father baffles and disgusts me. What is even more upsetting, though, is what he did to Ruth. The son called people to change the locks on the house (with all Ruth's belongings inside), pack up everything, and sell it. He cast Ruth and her family out in the middle of the pandemic without a word. All they had was their vehicle and the clothes on their backs. Meanwhile, Ruth's husband was stuck in Greece due to the pandemic and tragically passed away three weeks later.

Ruth and her oldest daughter had no choice but to start living in her car. They went to social services and tried to get housing, but they were denied because they had a vehicle. Social services put her in touch with various affordable housing organizations, but none of them would return her calls. This past winter they were able to join the Women's Hospitality Network, but besides that three-month respite, Ruth and her daughter have been living in their car for the last three and a half years. Each month, they collectively get $23 of food stamps. That is just an insult! Since Ruth is deaf in one ear, she can't work. While this made the interview very difficult and her daughter had to repeat many of our questions to Ruth, thankfully, it means she qualifies for SSI disability payments. This provides Ruth with just enough money to pay for car insurance, gas, and food.

Ruth is now sixty years old and her oldest daughter is thirty-nine. Going forward, they have no clear avenue to escape homelessness. Every housing organization Ruth has reached out to has been unresponsive. Ruth's life story really makes me angry with America's social services programs. After Ruth was hurt so much, she persevered to get married, start a family, and work an honest job for decades. Why should she feel that if "you want housing you need to be HIV positive or have a mental health issue?" Our government assistance programs failed Ruth in her time of crisis.

Ruth mentioned a few other details about her life that didn't quite fit into the chronology which I will mention here:

Ruth had five siblings who had to endure the same childhood struggles as she did. When Ruth ran away from home, she asked her nine-year-old sister to come with her, but her sister was too scared. She never had another opportunity to escape. She had it worse than Ruth as her four brothers also sexually abused her. Ruth shared that her father ended up getting her sister pregnant and then forced her to have an abortion. I simply don't have the words to express my sympathy.

During the interview, Ruth never mentioned much about her younger daughter, just that she has an apartment in Keyport and a daughter of her own. They are still close and Ruth visits as often as she can.

When Ruth is feeling down in the dumps though, religion has been her source of power. There were many times in her childhood when she contemplated suicide, but her belief was strong enough that she was able to keep living. Even now, Ruth attends church as often as she can and has unbreakable faith. No amount of misfortune can take that away from her.

The most depressing fact that Ruth shared with us is that she often feels extremely degraded in public. Just the other day, she went to a QuickChek to use the bathroom, and the workers there were extremely rude to her. They called her good for nothing and told her to get out. For Ruth and her daughter, this is a common occurrence. Ruth told us, "Instead of hearing our story, they look at the homeless and say they are spending money on drinks and drugs. I don't do any of that. I tell people if you don't know my story, don't judge me, but we get judged every day."

27

JBJ Soul Kitchen

It seemed as if everywhere I went in Red Bank, New Jersey, I heard about the Jon Bon Jovi Soul Kitchen. The three women I had interviewed and Kevin McGee all showered the organization with praise. After a few quick Google searches, I was impressed with the brilliance and complexity of the operation. I knew I had to go see it in action and talk to some of the staff. I was able to contact the Community Coordinator, Nicole Dorrity, and scheduled a meeting.

Our meeting was on a Thursday an hour before they opened. As soon as we arrived, I felt what I can only describe as a homey feeling. Outside was a large garden with plants and beautiful flowers everywhere. There were a couple of volunteers tending to the garden all of whom greeted us on our way in. Nicole happened to be outside and showed us around. Past the garden is outdoor seating under an overhang. What a view they have! The whole building felt extremely open with its huge glass windows that open into doors on nice days. The interior was extremely upbeat with a large window opening up into the kitchen. Nicole introduced us to the chefs, Emily and Chris, and then we sat down to talk.

The Jon Bon Jovi Soul Kitchen is a restaurant with a "dining with dignity" model. Anyone can come for a meal, and if they can't pay, they don't have to. Every guest is welcomed with a smile and treated with the same dignity and compassion. If a guest cannot afford food, they can volunteer to help as payment for their meal. There is a long list of tasks including coming early and helping set up the restaurant, organizing, cleaning, and gardening, to name just a few. Anyone who can pay is asked to "pay it forward" and donate $30 to sponsor a meal for the next person. The community supports those who are food insecure through donations.

When dining at the Soul Kitchen, everyone feels equal. It is difficult to tell who is food-insecure and who isn't, as they have all sorts of measures in place to ensure that it is completely anonymous. Additionally, (with permission) they often pair strangers to eat meals together. The idea is to foster inclusivity and connection in the community while being sensitive to everyone's financial position. For that reason, they call themselves a community restaurant and have all sorts of events to bring people together. The Soul Kitchen only has a few paid staff members; all other daily operations are covered by volunteers. Not only are there many who volunteer in exchange for meals, but tons of community members regularly volunteer for the organization. We met one amazing older woman who has been volunteering in the garden for almost a decade.

If any of the food-insecure customers request assistance, Nicole jumps into action to help. She has connections with lots of nearby organizations and is often able to connect them with organizations that fit their needs. She shared many stories in which she found people employment as a result of her job recommendations based on their experience volunteering at the Soul Kitchen. In some cases, they've come back years later able to pay for their own meal!

Nicole invited us to have dinner with her afterward, but as observant Jews, we had to decline as the food was not kosher. We did, however, agree to return on Sunday to meet the general manager and see the restaurant on its busiest day.

While we were on our way out, we saw Ruth and her daughter sit down for dinner. They were both dressed nicely and if we hadn't interviewed them, I'd never have guessed they were living in a vehicle. Here, they were treated with respect and dignity and I could see that in the way they carried themselves and how they sat upright. It was a brilliant demonstration of the power of the Soul Kitchen and the success of their methods.

Nicole told us that she had an event to attend on Sunday, but would tell the General Manager, Lou Morreale, to expect us. The restaurant was very busy when we arrived, but once things quieted down a little and Lou was free, he sat down with us. He bears a striking resemblance to Jon Bon Jovi, although Lou claims he is more often compared with Bon Jovi's father.

Lou has been involved in the Soul Kitchen since the very beginning. He is a friend of Bon Jovi and, because of his prior experience as a restaurant owner, jumped on the opportunity to volunteer at the Soul Kitchen back when they were first getting started. In 2014, Lou became General Manager and since then has been taking care of day-to-day operations. He has been essential to the opening of three new locations and is currently planning a fifth. Like so many I've met in the nonprofit world, Lou truly loves his job and takes pride in his work. He embodies their motto, "Happy are the hands that feed."

While Nicole told us everything about the Soul Kitchen's goals, Lou was able to give us a lot more information on the foundation as a whole. The Soul Kitchen is actually one part of the Jon Bon Jovi Soul Foundation which has been fighting poverty and homelessness all across America for almost twenty years. A whole book can be written just about how much Jon and Dorothea have done through the Soul Foundation. They are constantly searching for new and innovative projects to take under their wing and bring to new heights.

Most recently, the Soul Foundation is partnering with Soldier On and the New England Patriots to build twenty-one units of permanent affordable housing for veterans. Lou told us about the many dozens of projects they've pioneered over the years. I'll share just a few.

One of the foundation's earliest projects was their Soul Homes in Philadelphia. They partnered with Project Home to build 55 units of permanent affordable housing and provide health care, education, and job opportunities to all the residents. Just a few months ago, they completed another housing development with Project Home in Philadelphia, the Inn of Amazing Mercy. This building is a recovery house paired with addiction services designated specifically for homeless men and women suffering from drug abuse problems.

In partnership with Fulfill and Inspire NJ, the Soul Foundation opened the B.E.A.T. (bringing everyone all together) Center in Toms River. The goal of the center is exactly what Ellen had pointed out was needed, a one-stop shop location. The B.E.A.T. Center has a food bank, job training programs, mental health and addiction counseling, housing assistance programs, a Soul Kitchen restaurant, programs for senior citizens, and more. They cover almost every service one can imagine. Having all these organizations in one area makes it exponentially easier for homeless and near-homeless individuals to access the help they need.

Towards the beginning of the book, I spoke about the importance of the Code Blue program, which provides overnight housing to those experiencing homelessness on extremely cold winter nights. In partnership with the Pilgrim Baptist Church, the Soul Foundation founded the Hope and Comfort Warming Center in Red Bank. Throughout the winter, they can house and provide meals for over twenty men. In the summer, the location is used as a cooling house on days that are extremely hot. A local church is currently working to launch a women's warming center.

One of the amazing things about Red Bank is that all of the faith-based and community-based organizations work together to maximize their effects. The Soul Kitchen's hours are specifically tailored for this purpose. Since Lunch Break offers breakfast and lunch on weekdays, the Soul Kitchen covers dinner. Additionally, they are the only place in Red Bank that offers meals on Sundays.

The atmosphere of the restaurant is so positive that just sitting there was extremely uplifting. Despite the pouring rain outside, the flow of customers never stopped and they all received the same attention and respect from staff and other customers. Lou told us that they serve hundreds of customers each week, close to 60% of whom are food-insecure.

It was pleasant speaking with Lou and an hour passed in no time. At the end of our meeting, Lou explained that the core concept behind the Soul Kitchen is the idea of a community supporting its less fortunate. While the Soul Kitchen is an ingenious large-scale way to accomplish this, Lou said that each individual can accomplish the same mission by just talking to people and making sure they feel heard and respected.

28

Results

After reading through a year of my life and the collective four hundred sixty years of the lives of those whom I've interviewed, we can finally get around to answering the fundamental questions of this book. Let's go one at a time.

How do people become homeless?

Sudden Disasters

When near-homeless individuals experience a sudden disaster, they are often thrust into homelessness. These disasters can materialize in many forms: natural disasters, the loss of a family member, a vehicle breaking down, an injury, or an illness. Without adequate preparation, this could drain their savings and sometimes prevent them from working. Insurance payments often come in way too late or cover only a fraction of the damages.

Larry was driven into a depression after his stepmother tragically passed. He lost his job at the car wash and drugs became his coping mechanism. While this didn't quite drive him into homelessness, it tore away his safety net. His father lost the house, and Larry and his cousins were on their own.

James Alai was torn down by three consecutive sudden disasters. The first was a devastating jaw injury that forced James to take time off from his job. While he was recovering, his younger brother died suddenly in a terrible car accident. A few months later, their apartment was flooded as a result of Superstorm Sandy. James was not able to handle all of these tragedies emotionally in such quick succession and fell apart.

Ellen's car was rear-ended and totaled only a few weeks before Superstorm Sandy. Insurance only paid for a portion of the cost of a new car, but she needed a vehicle to get to work. Ellen had to dig into her savings to get a new car. When the hurricane hit, Ellen was not equipped financially to survive the disaster.

Ruth was driven into homelessness after the man she was taking care of passed and his son kicked them out of the house and took all their belongings. Meanwhile, her husband was stuck in Greece in the middle of a global pandemic. Ruth had no way to make money and could not afford to rent.

Dysfunctional Social Culture

In a functional social culture, children learn the ability to self-regulate from those around them. Self-regulation is the ability to manage your own behaviors and emotions. This allows people to modulate their reactions (like anger or sadness), focus on a task, control their impulses, and behave normally in social situations. When they have to make complicated decisions, they are able to think logically, weigh all of their options, seek counsel (if necessary), and choose the best option.

When parents are negligent or do not have the ability to self-regulate, they cannot endow their children with all of the social and emotional skills they need to make it in the world. These children are hardwired to feel anxious and to make impulsive decisions. Similarly, when a child grows up in an unpredictable and stressful environment, they often experience psychological limitations that prevent them from thinking clearly and planning ahead. This manifests in many forms including symptoms similar to ADHD, mood swings, and mental health issues. The problem becomes generational as the children who are never taught to self-regulate quickly become the next generation of parents.

Both of Larry's parents were alcoholic and abusive. They never gave him the attention or love that a child requires. He didn't have a single moment of security and his brain was constantly on high alert. His father was likely bipolar and had frequent bursts of anger. In this environment, Larry never learned the ability to control his emotions. As a result, he had frequent temper tantrums in school and was bullied. Although he graduated high school with a job and a trade, he was not prepared psychologically to enter the world.

James Alai's father was very callous and largely absent in his child-hood, so instead, his mother primarily raised him. The problem is that she suffers from depression and severe agoraphobia. When he was faced with his huge challenge, he was unable to self-regulate and fell into a deep depression. He used morphine to numb his mind and developed a drug addiction. During our interview, James pointed out that he "still has the emotions of a teenager."

Carlos grew up in a chaotic environment as he was juggled between his father's abusive home, various foster houses, juvenile detention centers, and the street. I'd even go as far as to say that Carlos never had a parental figure. He was motivated by physical power and independence. Drugs and alcohol were always in his life and it is no surprise that he followed the same path as everyone around him. Today, Carlos still struggles to learn how to self-regulate and fit into society.

Manny's parents got divorced when he was young and he lived with his mother. She had severe mental health problems her entire life and Manny was never taught basic social skills. He was unable to get along with other kids his age and his teachers. Manny was kicked out of his schools because of this and his education fell behind. All the while, he felt like a social outcast as he was exploring his sexuality. When he started over in Cape May, he got too involved with the partying while trying to fit in. Instead of self-regulating in a traditional way, he used drugs to ignore his emotions. Manny never stopped making impulsive decisions and based on his reaction to his carrots being stolen, he clearly still cannot control his emotions.

James Vick grew up without a father present and instead, followed the example of the boys around him in school. All of the older kids were doing drugs and partying, so James followed suit. Every decision he made was impulsive, including having a child at age fourteen. From there, he followed the example of his own father and eventually abandoned his own child as well.

Ruth escaped her abusive parents when she was only eleven. Until her future husband took her in, she lived in abusive and unpredictable conditions. Everything and everyone was hostile and not to be trusted. It was only due to her husband's compassion and protection that she was able to persevere and beat the odds for so long.

Abusive Upbringings

Children who are abused not only feel the effect of a dysfunctional social culture as they have no trusted adults in their lives, but the psychological damage can be much more pervasive. Head injuries can lead to physical brain damage which could have a wide range of effects depending on where the damage is. It is difficult to predict the precise impacts of abuse on a person, but overall those who experience child abuse are more likely to use alcohol and drugs, suffer from physical health problems, experience decreased cognitive function, have low self-esteem, struggle in social situations, develop mental health problems, and experience PTSD.

As a result of the abuse Larry faced, he struggled socially, felt low self-esteem, and was unable to overcome his psychological struggles. He lost many jobs due to anger issues and was unable to make it in society. Instead, he used drugs as a coping mechanism.

Carlos developed an inferiority complex and sought power throughout his childhood. His half-siblings all teased him and he desired to lord over them. When he finally had the chance to gain independence, he took it. He separated from his father and promptly became homeless.

Ruth, again, is an exception. Despite all the abuse she suffered at the hands of her father and her boss, she was taken in by her future husband and kept safe. There she was able to develop into a functioning person. She held a job, started a family, and raised three children.

Lack of Affordable Housing

While it sounds juvenile to say that the reason people become homeless is because they can't afford a house, it is a real problem. For many near-homeless individuals, the majority of their income goes directly to rent. This is a huge financial strain on them. If there is an emergency and they need to find a new place to live, it can be extremely difficult to find a new apartment in their price range and they might have to stay in a hotel or motel until they can find permanent residence.

After Superstorm Sandy, Ellen's apartment was practically uninhabitable, but she had no better option than inhaling toxic mold. If you could find an apartment, the prices were over double what they had been a year before, and Ellen had already been spending more than half her income on rent. Because of the unsafe conditions in her apartment, Ellen fell ill and lost her job. After that, she couldn't even pay rent.

After Rose and her son were evicted from their apartment after a bedbug dispute, they couldn't find an affordable apartment. While it was originally a temporary measure to stay at a motel, they ended up spending the next four and a half years there and were unable to save up money. After Rose's son had a few slow weeks at work in a row, they couldn't even afford the motel and Rose had to move into her vehicle.

After Ruth was kicked out of her apartment by a despicable landlord and all her assets were stolen, she had no place to stay. Ruth and her daughter had to move into her car and have been there ever since. They did not have enough money to afford an apartment, and no shelter would take them in.

Lack of a Safety Net

In my personal experience, when someone comes upon hard times, their family, friends, and community step up to assist. Unfortunately, not everyone has that "safety net," and in emergencies, they have to fend for themselves. In the case of a flood, they may not have a friend whose couch they can crash on. If their car needs maintenance, they may not be able to get a ride. If they fall ill, no one will deliver them soup. If they have a hard day or week, they might not have anyone to talk to about it. In even more extreme circumstances, they might not be able to keep their heads above water and be forced into homelessness.

The summer after Manny left Manhattan, he decided to go to Cape May and work to save up some money so that he could buy an apartment in Harrisburg. His plan was to stay with his father so that he could put some money in the bank, but his father refused. He had effectively cut ties with his mother, so he was stuck. He ended up couch-hopping for a while before splitting rent with someone he met. When the summer ended, he couldn't afford an apartment and had to continue couch-hopping in Philadelphia. While he wasn't living on the streets, he was practically homeless during this time.

When Ellen's house was taken over by toxic mold, if a friend had been able to take her in right away, the story would have gone very differently. Instead of falling ill and losing her job, Ellen might have been able to work hard and survive the disaster. Eventually, she could have regathered her thoughts and made the difficult decision to flee to an area with a lower cost of living. Unfortunately, Ellen received no such aid until it was too late.

After Ruth lost her housing and all of her possessions, she had no one to fall back on. Her husband was stuck in Greece and no one was able to temporarily house Ruth and her daughter. Instead, they went straight to their vehicle where they are still living today.

Why can't they escape homelessness?

Lack of Affordable Housing

Not only can the lack of affordable housing be the catalyst that drives someone into homelessness, but it is also a major obstacle for those working to escape homelessness. In America, there is simply not enough affordable housing. Almost every article I've read and every conversation I've had points towards homelessness being primarily a housing problem. In New Jersey, it takes years of waiting to even be entered into a database of those who need housing.

Without access to affordable housing, those experiencing homelessness cannot afford a suitable apartment. On the streets, it is difficult to save up money. Without aid from charities, many don't even receive enough from social services for food and clothing. Those who have cars have the added expense of gas and frequent repairs; they funnel all of their money into an asset that quickly depreciates in value. Even if one is able to put aside money month after month, where should they store it? It is extremely difficult for someone experiencing homelessness to open a bank account, so unless they have one from before they were homeless, they have to carry their savings with them. It is unlikely that one can accumulate a meaningful amount of money without it being stolen.

The men we spoke with at the Canright House were not struggling with this problem, because they were already being housed by the program. They all mentioned that they were extremely lucky that there was a house specifically designated for HIV-positive men. For all of the interviews we had outside of a shelter, though, lack of affordable housing is the reason they are still experiencing homelessness.

Drug and Alcohol Addiction

Many experiencing homelessness resort to substance abuse as a coping mechanism. Unable to self-regulate, they dull their brains to live with their pain. Since these substances are so addictive and mind-altering, they can easily get hooked. Eventually, they can't live without taking drugs. Motivated by the fear of withdrawal, they sink deeper and deeper. In order to support their addiction, they scam, steal, and rob innocent people without any qualms. In their mind, it is literally do or die. This is a very dangerous cycle to enter and requires herculean strength to escape. The most common outcomes are overdose or fentanyl poisoning.

It is critical to realize that these unfortunate outcomes are symptoms of the problems mentioned above, not the problem in and of itself. Larry did not become homeless because of a drug addiction, he became addicted to drugs because he was abused as a child, never learned how to self-regulate, and lost his family at a young age. James Alai was prescribed morphine as a pain medication after a serious injury. His mother had mental health issues and his father was negligent; as a result, he never learned how to handle his emotions. When his brother passed, he continued to use morphine (and later heroin) for his emotional rather than physical pain. Carlos grew up in a community where drug use was extremely common. He followed in the paths of the men around him without even a thought. The problem was rooted in his upbringing and community, not with him personally. I can keep going with Manny and James Vick, but the point is clear, drug abuse is a symptom of the problem, not the fundamental problem itself.

This is an extremely critical point because the misconception that homelessness is a drug problem is not only incorrect but extremely dangerous. The three people I interviewed who didn't have any bouts with substance abuse are being neglected because they don't match the stereotype of the homeless. The reason they aren't in shelters is that most shelters have become rehab programs for those with drug addictions and mental health problems. As a result of the misconception above, much of the efforts to help the homeless are being guided to one demographic and people like Rose, Ellen, and Ruth are unable to get the assistance they need. This mistake is a distraction from the real underlying causes of homelessness and has practical ramifications that hurt men and women experiencing homelessness who have never had any substance abuse problems.

Lack of Assistance from Social Services

In many cases, Social Services does not provide enough money for those experiencing homelessness to survive. Even Rose, who worked until she turned sixty, did not make enough from Social Security to support even a simple lifestyle. Ruth and her daughter collectively receive $23 a month in food stamps and Ellen told us that numbers this low are not uncommon. It is evident that America's Social Services programs are not providing enough assistance for those experiencing homelessness to even survive without the assistance of charities, much less save up money to escape poverty. Instead, private nonprofits are taking over and doing incredible work in their respective areas. Organizations like Lunch Break and Interfaith Neighbors are saving lives every single day with their multitude of programs. All of the men and women I interviewed made it clear that without these charitable efforts, there was no chance they would be able to survive.

What could be done to help?

More Affordable Housing

Yes, after a year of work, one of my insights is that the solution to people not having houses is to build them houses. There is a huge lack of affordable housing and the only way to solve that is to build more affordable houses. Many of the organizations I've met with are building houses on the side, but it is extremely expensive, complicated, and slow. Additionally, these projects have only been possible due to government funding or donations from large corporations.

The good news is that year over year the government has been steadily increasing funding for the Department of Housing and Urban Development. This money goes directly to building new affordable housing units for low-income and homeless individuals. I hope that this money is spent responsibly.

Currently, tax breaks and building incentives are offered to home-builders if they set aside a certain percentage of their portfolio for affordable housing. In addition to the expansion of this system, increased government funding for the affordable housing building programs of nonprofits like Interfaith Neighbors could make a huge difference.

Short-Term Liquidity Assistance

Sudden disasters are a frequent cause of homelessness. Sometimes people don't have enough savings or a community to fall back on when they are in a pinch. If a large-scale organization existed to give small low-interest loans to low-income individuals in an emergency situation, they might be able to stay afloat during this difficult time. This would be comparable to a microloan program for low-income Americans to weather tough economic times. Let's look at it hypothetically.

Imagine a situation where someone's car broke down and needs to be repaired. They don't have enough savings to cover the repair. This organization would loan them the money for the repairs so that they could continue to work and make money. They might have to take public transport for a few days, but once the car is fixed, their life can return to normal. Over the next twelve months, they would repay the loan in installments. Instead of incurring serious credit card debt which would quickly snowball or losing their job, this organization would stop the problem in its tracks.

Naturally, in the case of a large-scale natural disaster, the demand would be incredibly high. The government can direct money to this organization and loosen restrictions. All of the money would be going directly to support the day-to-day costs of those affected by the disaster. Ellen would be able to remove the mold from her apartment or find a new place to stay. She wouldn't have gotten sick and would be able to continue working. After a few months, things would have returned to some degree of normal and Ellen could begin repaying the loans.

Social Services Expansion

Since Social Services does not provide enough money to those in need, it is clear changes must be made. The dollar amounts of payments must be increased as the amount supplied by Social Services is simply not enough to survive on. Also, the amount they provide must be relative to the cost of living of the state. Living costs in New Jersey are much more expensive than in West Virginia, but Social Services does not take this into consideration. Faith-based and community-based nonprofits (like Interfaith Neighbors, Lunch Break, and the Soul Foundation) pick up the slack. If incredible organizations with proven track records could be partially government-funded, they could ensure that everyone in their community has access to food and clothing.

Building Social and Emotional Skills in Children and Young Adults

As Mr. McEvilly explained to me in my first meeting of Project Unhoused, it is exponentially easier to prevent someone from being homeless in the first place than it is to bring them out of homelessness. With that being said, the ability to self-regulate is the most significant common factor that I've noticed among the people I've interviewed. If the children of a certain community—generation after generation—are not taught how to control their emotions, it is extremely difficult for them to succeed in life. One avenue to assisting our community is ensuring that every young adult enters the world equipped with the emotional tools and the confidence to chase their dreams.

While the other solutions suggested require top-down approaches in which the government makes policy changes that will affect our communities, this would be more of a grassroots program. With all that I've learned this last year as our inspiration, my family has been partnering with Rabbi Ricky Cohen, to form a nonprofit organization named Advance to hopefully fill this void in our community.

The purpose of the program is to instill in young adults the self-confidence and self-love to make difficult long-term decisions at a pivotal point in their lives. The program begins with a three-day overnight retreat in which each participant learns more about themselves and their interests through a project-based learning curriculum. Then, over the next two months, there are virtual group meetings with Rabbi Ricky Cohen who teaches the young adults life skills and instills within them an unshakable sense of self. Additionally, each participant is paired with a mentor in a similar field to that which they identified as a passion of theirs. At the end of the program, there is a gala dinner in which everyone presents their progress and what they have been working on. This can range widely from deciding which major to choose in college to starting a new business. Everyone will have chosen a different path. Potential investors and partners will be invited for those looking to start businesses and potential employers for those looking for jobs.

After leaving the program, each graduate will have the next actionable step in their development, the tools to persevere through any setbacks, and a long-term relationship with a mentor in a similar field to that which they are pursuing whom they can go to for guidance. It is our hope that this program will continue to expand to communities across the country and make a difference for the next generation of young adults.

What can we do?

The most actionable way to assist the homeless is through volunteer work and donations. Many organizations run seasonal drives for items like clothing, canned foods, gifts, etc... Donating these items is a very helpful and convenient way to help. Also, almost all the nonprofits I've met with have volunteer opportunities. They have a constant demand, and the more hands on deck the better. It is transformative to have face-to-face contact with those you are helping and this is the reason why I love the winter clothing distributions so much. Additionally, I would highly recommend making a visit to the Jon Bon Jovi Soul Kitchen and spending time with community members from different backgrounds.

I completely understand that not everyone has enough free time to dedicate to helping those experiencing homelessness, and there are so many other problems clamoring for our attention. My advice to everyone, including the people who can't take upon themselves more time commitments, is a change in perspective.

As Ruth so beautifully described, we cannot judge people without knowing their stories. We should not look down upon those who fell upon hard times. We should realize that we don't know what they've been through. How does this materialize? Instead of looking the other way as we pass someone experiencing homelessness, we might at least give a smile. Maybe we could greet them with a nice "hello" or "good afternoon." It is only a small gesture, but it makes a huge difference to the mindsets of both parties. If everyone Ruth and her daughter had met had greeted them warmly, she might have gone to sleep each night happy with a renewed sense of self-worth. That alone is of immeasurable value.

29

Conclusion

L ooking back over the last year, I am amazed by the growth I've exhibited in terms of maturity and understanding others. Before Project Unhoused, I was stuck in my own life. It wasn't like everything revolved around me, but my experiences and thoughts were all centered around my family, friends, community, or interests. I didn't spend much time dwelling on things I wasn't directly involved with. When I read or learned about others' lives, I extracted specific lessons and incorporated them into my life, but the soul behind the experiences was lost on me. In the interviews I conducted, though, I delved deep into the psyche of those who were opening up to me. I didn't just hear their words, I tried to live through their stories. It only occurred to me later that this is the difference between sympathy and empathy. I attribute this emotional development to this new perspective through which I view others and our absolute interconnectedness.

That is not to say that I have plateaued; from both an organizational and personal standpoint, this is just the beginning. The primary goal of this book is to educate Americans on our homelessness problem to remove common misconceptions and stereotypes. I hope that the fresh perspective I've shared has refined your understanding of how people become homeless and how we as a country are letting down our less fortunate. All of the profits from book sales and donations will go directly into fueling the next stages of Project Unhoused.

After publication, I have no plans to slow down. This winter I will continue to collect and distribute winter clothing directly to the homeless and near-homeless in our community. In partnership with the Ocean Township City Council, we will have four municipal drop-off locations and stronger local advertising. Mark Wilson and I are beyond excited to jump back into action!

Having completed eight interviews with formerly unhoused Americans from very different backgrounds, I covered only a relatively small sample size. Going forwards, I intend to continue my interviews and will write up summaries which I will share through my website. Additionally, provided we raise enough money through donations, my dream is to provide monthly stipends to help some of the people I've interviewed whom I identify really need extra money and will be putting it to good use. A recurring payment like this could help them afford food, rent, or build savings.

Lastly, I have an ambitious idea which I would like your help with. I have only been able to have a very limited impact in my geographical region. All of the interviews and distributions I've conducted have been in Asbury Park or Red Bank, New Jersey. I do not have the ability to expand countrywide on my own, but I am certain that there are like minded youth across the country who would jump on an opportunity to assist people experiencing homelessness in their communities.

The problem is that it is very difficult to start anything from scratch; however, I have already built the infrastructure, the hardest part. My idea is a program that high-schoolers across America can bring to their own schools. They would raise money to purchase (at cost) pre-made bags filled with items I've learned over the last year that are essential for those living on the streets. Then, they could have an event handing out these bags to those who need them most in their communities. I've already negotiated wholesale pricing for all of the items and am ready to supply completed packages.

I will be advertising this program through my social media channels, but I need your help to push this further. If you could recommend any students or schools that are interested in such a partnership, that would be incredibly helpful in expanding our efforts to a completely new scale! If you are a student interested in bringing this program to your school, reach out to me. If you are a parent or grandparent, talk to your child/grandchild about this opportunity. If you are an aunt or an uncle, mention Project Unhoused at your next family gathering.

Below is a QR code for my Venmo and website if you would like to support these efforts or contact me.

Venmo

Website

Acknowledgement

To Donna Elms, the program supervisor at the Winifred-Canright House: Your enormous heart and smile are unique and your dedication to the community is beyond inspiring. I simply do not understand how you carve the time to attend college and raise a family, too. You have been instrumental to the writing of this book and I cannot thank you enough. Your alacrity and the joy with which you help others have made working with you a true pleasure.

To Kevin McGee, director of operations at Lunch Break: From our first meeting, I got the impression that you were as excited about this project as I was. Immediately after we met, you threw your full weight behind Project Unhoused, catapulting us to new heights. You epitomize the idea that if someone chooses a job they love, they'll never work a day in their life. Despite always being busy, you never seem to slow down or shirk responsibility, and I've never seen you without a smile on your face.

To Cherry Elliot and Mark Wilson, both of whom have been essential to our winter clothing distributions: Cherry, thank you for jumping on this opportunity to help. The degree to which you go out of your way to help others is clear. You are the queen of Asbury Park and everyone knows it! Mark, my God-Second-Cousin, there is never a boring moment when you help us run a distribution. You somehow know and bring the good out of everyone. What a gift.

To Mayor Napolitani and the Ocean Township City Council: The speed with which you replied to all of my emails and your willingness to meet with me and give your guidance is representative of your supreme focus on listening to and assisting all citizens of your city. Your help with advertising and collecting has been incredibly helpful.

To all of those I've met fighting homelessness in our community: Thank you for providing me guidance and introducing me to your peers. The nonprofit world is wholesome and collaborative, and you all welcomed me like family.

To my Rabbis, Abraham Ashkenazi and Rabbi Ricky Cohen: Without our learning, I never would have reached the level a year ago where I could go through with a project this ambitious. Thank you for your undying support and guidance in all matters. Our daily learning sharpens my mind and opens my heart. I would not be here without you.

To my friends: Thank you for all of your assistance with raising money, donating clothing, and conducting distributions. While almost all of your help was behind the scenes, it has been essential to the success of this project and the writing of this book.

To my family: Thank you to everyone who donated, dropped off clothing, or helped with spreading the word about my project. Thank you to my siblings, Noah and Mimi, for their support and advice. A special thank you to my Aunt Ida and Uncle Jon Levy for their help with almost every aspect of the project including fundraising, advertising, conducting distributions, editing, and cover art design. Your unique perspectives and keen eyes have proven invaluable. Thank you for never holding back.

To my editor, Sally Taylor Tawil: You have truly been essential to the writing of this book. Every one of your comments was spot on. Despite the time crunch and all that you have on your plate, it felt like you dropped everything to work on my project. Thank you for your commitment and expertise.

To my parents, who have been paramount to every aspect of this journey: From when I first pitched the idea at the dinner table, you have empowered me to pursue my ideas regardless of how unlikely they may have seemed. You were my first donors and briefed me before and after my first meetings. You listened to and critiqued every draft text, email, speech, and eventually chapter. You can easily make the argument that you've spent enough time sitting on the couch in the living room discussing Project Unhoused with me to constitute a full-time job. Without your support, advice, and your car, none of this would have been possible.

Images

Interview #1: Larry

Interview #2: James Alai

Meeting Cherry at Dunkin' Donuts

Distribution #1

Interview #3: Carlos

Billie Weise and me

Distribution #2

Distribution #2

Interview #4: Manny

Interview #5: James Vick

Distribution #3: From left to right—my father, me, Cherry, and Sahrue

Distribution #3

Kevin McGee and me

Interview #6: Rose

Distribution #4: Back row left to right—my father, Mark Wilson, and me

Distribution #4

Ocean Township City Council Meeting: From left to right—Councilwoman Kelly Terry, Mayor John Napolitani, Me, State Senator Declan O'Scanlon, Councilman Robert Acerra, and Councilwoman Margie Donlon

Eileen Mizrahi and me

Distribution #5: From left to right—me, Mark Wilson, my father, and Joseph Aboudi

Distribution #5

Distribution #5

Interview #8: Ruth and her daughter (on the right)

JBJ Soul Kitchen: From left to right—Nicole Dorrity, me, and Chris Ross

Advance Launch Night: From left to right—my brother, Noah; my mother, Dyan; my father, Izzy; me; and my sister, Mimi

Advance Launch Event

Advance Meeting: From left to right—my mother, my sister, my brother, Rabbi Ricky Cohen, my father, and me

Advance Event

Bibliography

1. https://today.yougov.com/topics/politics/articles-reports/2022/05/17/american-attitudes-on-homelessness-poll
2. https://www.apa.org/monitor/jun01/cogcentral
3. https://www.mind.org.uk/information-support/types-of-mental-health-problems/bipolar-disorder/causes-of-bipolar/
4. https://adamsbroomfieldda.org/Fentanyl-Fact-Sheet
5. https://invisiblepeople.tv/cold-truth-hypothermia-is-taking-homeless-peoples-lives/
6. https://nhchc.org/clinical-practice/diseases-and-conditions/cold-related-injuries/
7. https://www.na.org/?ID=ips-an-an-IP1
8. https://csgjusticecenter.org/publications/after-the-sentence-more-consequences/national-snapshot/
9. https://www.prisonpolicy.org/reports/housing.html
10. https://www.cdc.gov/hiv/basics/livingwithhiv/newly-diagnosed.html
11. https://hellopoetry.com/poem/1554798/alone-the-walls/
12. https://www.priorygroup.com/mental-health/drug-induced-psychosis
13. https://www.senatorgopal.com/gopal_announces_250_000_homelessness_prevention_grant_to_social_services_nonprofit_in_asbury_park
14. https://www.fema.gov/blog/remembering-hurricane-sandy-10-

years-later

15. https://dep.nj.gov/sandy-10/

16. https://www.nyc.gov/content/sandytracker/pages/overview

17. https://www.usnews.com/news/best-states/rankings/opportunity/affordability/cost-living?sort=rank-desc

18. https://www.healthcare.gov/glossary/federal-poverty-level-fpl/

19. https://livingwage.mit.edu/states/34

20. https://www.njspotlightnews.org/video/more-than-2-million-people-in-nj-live-in-poverty-with-no-federal-support/

About the Author

Zac Levy is a student at High Technology High School in Lincroft, New Jersey. In addition to his humanitarian work, he is a graduate of the Rutgers University Quarknet Program in particle physics and quantum computing. Levy is working with Dr. Matthew Rosenberg in the lab of Professor David Tank at Princeton University, conducting research in the fields of neuroscience and biophysics. In line with his beliefs as an Orthodox Jew, he dedicates time to learning Judaic Studies with his Rabbis every morning and night. In his free time, Levy enjoys playing tennis and chess.

You can connect with me on:
- https://www.projectunhoused.com
- https://gofund.me/7ea00a9d
- https://www.instagram.com/project_unhoused

Made in the USA
Columbia, SC
19 August 2024

8a8e6401-0bff-4180-955e-32b695e6bda1R01